THE STORY OF CHAMPAGNE

LUXURY EDITION

For Kitty

Previously published as The Treasures of Champagne by Carlton Books in 2016 and Champagne: Wine of Kings and King of Wines by Welbeck Publishing in 2021.
This edition published by OH
An Imprint of HEADLINE PUBLISHING GROUP LIMITED

1

Cataloguing in Publication Data is available from the British Library

ISBN 978-1-03542-794-9

Printed and bound in China by Toppan Leefung Printing Ltd.

Headline's policy is to use papers that are natural, renewable and recyclable products and made from wood grown in well-managed forests and other controlled sources. The logging and manufacturing processes are expected to conform to the environmental regulations of the country of origin.

Editorial: Heather Boisseau / Matt Tomlinson
Design: Russell Knowles
Production: Rachel Burgess
Picture Research: Paul Langan

HEADLINE PUBLISHING GROUP LIMITED
An Hachette UK Company
Carmelite House
50 Victoria Embankment,
London EC4Y 0DZ

The authorised representative in the EEA is Hachette Ireland
8 Castlecourt Centre
Dublin 15, D15 XTP3, Ireland (email: info@hbgi.ie)

www.headline.co.uk
www.hachette.co.uk

THE STORY OF
CHAMPAGNE
LUXURY EDITION

THE ULTIMATE GUIDE TO THE WORLD'S
MOST FAMOUS SPARKLING WINE

TOM BRUCE-GARDYNE

OH

CONTENTS

THE ESSENTIALS OF CHAMPAGNE - 011

THE HISTORY OF CHAMPAGNE - 027

ON THE CHAMPAGNE ROUTE - 053

SPARKLING WINES OF THE WORLD - 119

CULTURE AND TRADITIONS - 137

INTRODUCTION

'Think pleasure, think parties, think celebration ... think champagne' has been the mantra of this most beguiling drink for centuries. We can all picture an ice-cold bottle plucked from the fridge, the foil ripped off and the wire cage removed. A brief pause of anticipation as the cork slowly emerges, and then that joyous 'pop' – signalling the party has truly begun.

The release of pressure unlocks the energy in the bottle, creating around a million bubbles in each glass according to scientific research. What the science explains as well is that the escaping CO2 tickles not just our tongue but also a valve in our tummy, propelling the alcohol into the bloodstream and up to the brain. To achieve the same buzz with still wine takes that much longer, or a serious workout on the dance floor. With champagne the bubbles do the dancing for you.

Other sparkling wines will give you the same effect, but there is something special about champagne. It is a word loaded with symbolism around sensuality, glamour and decadence. Champagne needs to be a luxury, or else it loses meaning. When Woolworth's sold it for £5 under its 'Worth It!' label in a publicity stunt some years ago, anyone given a bottle might have adapted that hoary old catchphrase of L'Oréal and decided 'it's because I'm not worth it'. Yet, of course, plenty of champagne brands know how to exploit the idea of being 'reassuringly expensive' and part of that celebrity lifestyle to which we allegedly aspire.

But cut through the marketing froth, and there's a fascinating story to champagne, not least how those bubbles got there in the first place. To set the scene, *The Story of Champagne* begins with the winemaking process and a brief history. For many years it was a complete mystery how and why champagne sparkled in this relatively cool corner of north-east France on the edge of planet wine. Was it something in the earth or in the stars? Or was it some ancient curse that caused endless bottles to shatter under the pressure? Eventually the Champenoise came to realize those fiendish bubbles were their greatest asset.

The modern era saw the rise of the great Champagne Houses, and their individual stories are continued in the middle part of the book. Beyond the big, familiar names lie some huge cooperatives that now have sizeable brands of their own. And behind them are the thousands of growers who tend the vines and perhaps dream of making their own wine. Those with land in the right place and sufficient self-belief and passion are doing just that with a myriad of grower champagnes that really do express the terroir of their vineyards.

Next there's an exploration of some of the myriad sparkling wines that champagne has inspired, from New Zealand to California's Napa Valley. There has been the phenomenal success of Italian prosecco and the rise of English sparkling wine that may one day become champagne's most serious rival. The final part of the book looks at the culture of champagne and how it has been refracted through the lens of cinema, art and literature. Throughout *The Story of Champagne* the aim is to celebrate this extraordinary wine in images as much as words, plundering the region's rich archive to bring the story alive.

Tom Bruce-Gardyne

1

THE ESSENTIALS OF CHAMPAGNE

The vineyards of champagne and the decision to focus on three grape varieties has been a slow evolution over centuries, as has the winemaking process. Today it is the most valuable and well-protected wine region in the world, while the predominant style of champagne has shifted from a late Victorian sweetness to bone dry.

THE CHAMPAGNE REGION

To the English the undulating slopes and famous chalky soils of the champagne region are reminiscent of the South Downs of Sussex and Kent. From a geological point of view this makes perfect sense because the Downs are a continuation of champagne, separated only by the Channel.

The Romans christened the region Campania, after the southern Italian province, and the name evolved into Champagne. The region starts in the Marne valley, just 35 miles east of Paris, and extends north of Reims and as far south as the outlying district of the Aube, just beyond the northern tip of Burgundy. Within this wide perimeter that covers five *départements* – Marne, Aisne, Aube, Haute-Marne and Seine-en-Marne – are 319 villages currently blessed with the right to produce champagne.

Around these villages the countryside can appear a complete monoculture with nothing but row upon row of manicured vines angled to catch the maximum sunlight. They are subdivided into neat parcels such that every available scrap of land in the *appellation's* 34,500 hectares is planted. In between the villages, however, are large forests and swathes of farmland whose crops can only look on with envy at the carefully tended and immensely profitable vineyards of Champagne.

That the word 'champagne' should be considered a unique geographic region and not just a particular style of sparkling wine has been crucial to the wine's success. Had the Champenois failed to map out the *appellation* and then defend it vigorously around the world, this quintessential luxury fizz would have become as generic as Yorkshire pudding. As a number of the big Champagne Houses have proved, you can produce a fine imitation elsewhere using the same process and the exact same grapes. But if you want to make champagne you can do so only in the eponymous region. That is what the French have long maintained, and today just about everyone agrees with them. The only exceptions are a few, die-hard Americans who continue to produce domestic 'champagne' for the US market only.

Within the Champagne region are five key areas, which, running north to south, start with:

THE MONTAGNE DE REIMS

Maybe the French were being *ironique*, but you don't need crampons or oxygen to reach the 275m summit of this upland plateau between Reims and Épernay which is capped with a thickly wooded national park. The region is famed for its pinot noir that accounts for 40% of plantings compared to 36% for pinot meunier and 24% for chardonnay. Beneath the trees, the northern slopes are carpeted with vines all the way round to the Grand Cru villages of Verzenay, Verzy and Sillery to the north-east. While to the south are the villages of Ambonnay, Louvois and Bouzy, also Grand Cru, which produce a slightly richer version of pinot noir than the firmer, more angular styles to the north.

Opposite: Grapes soaking up the sunshine in a vineyard in Montagne de Reims.

Below: Detailed maps of the Champagne region, the upper one focusing on the villages, vineyards and Champagne Houses of the Montagne de Reims and Éperon de Bouzy and the lower one on the Vallée de la Marne.

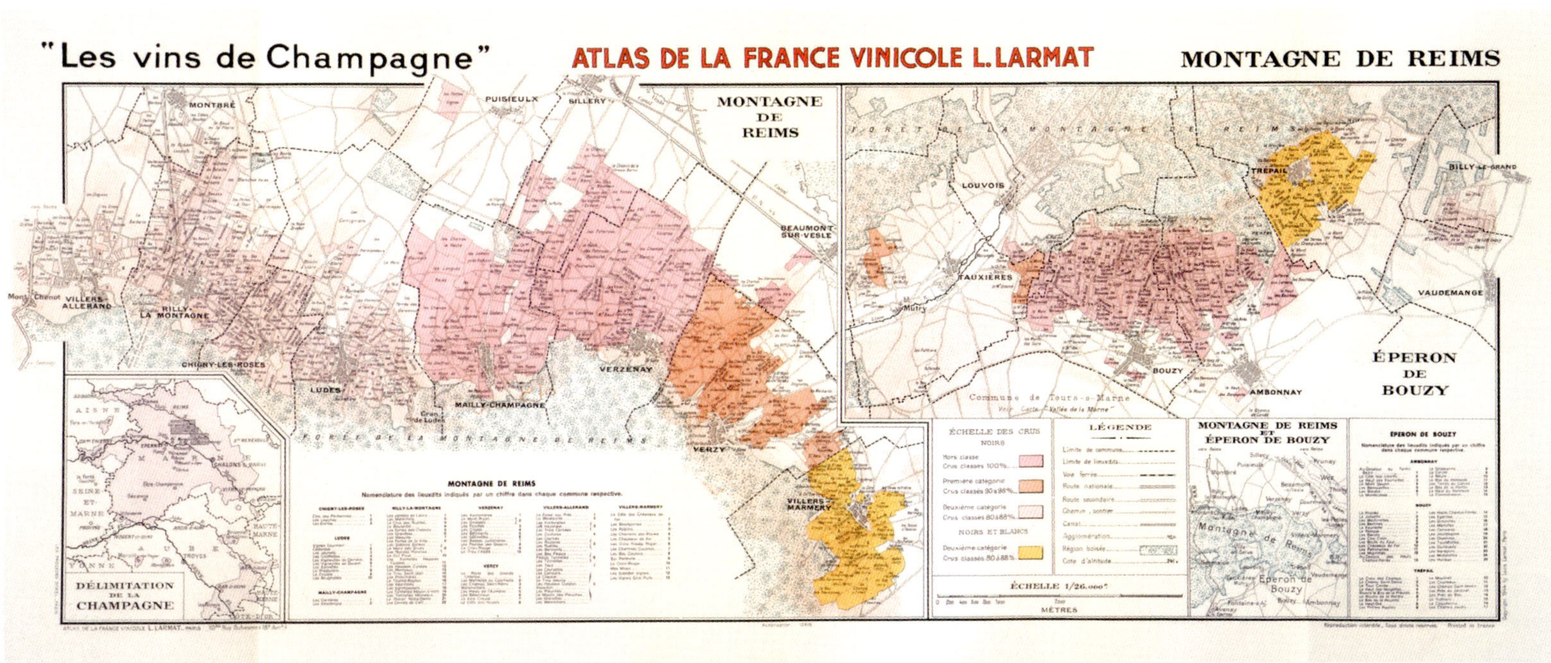

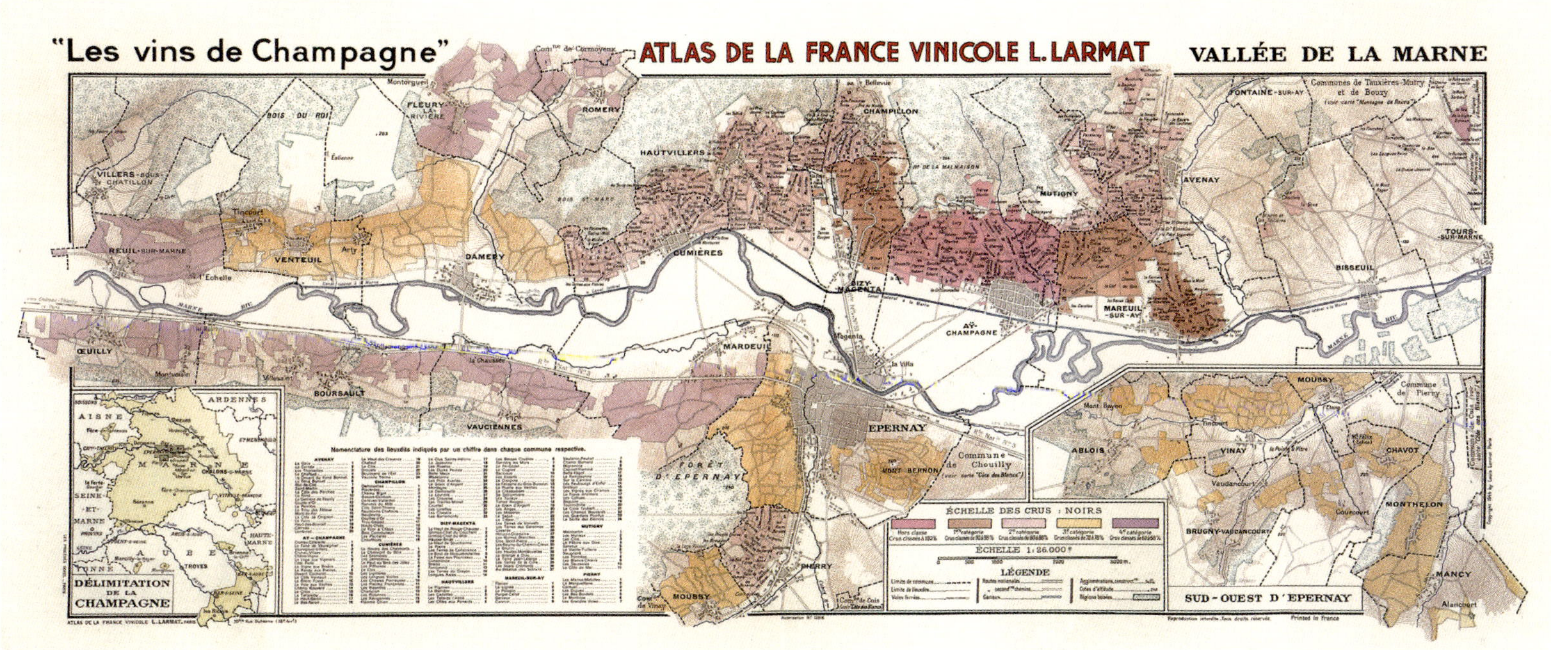

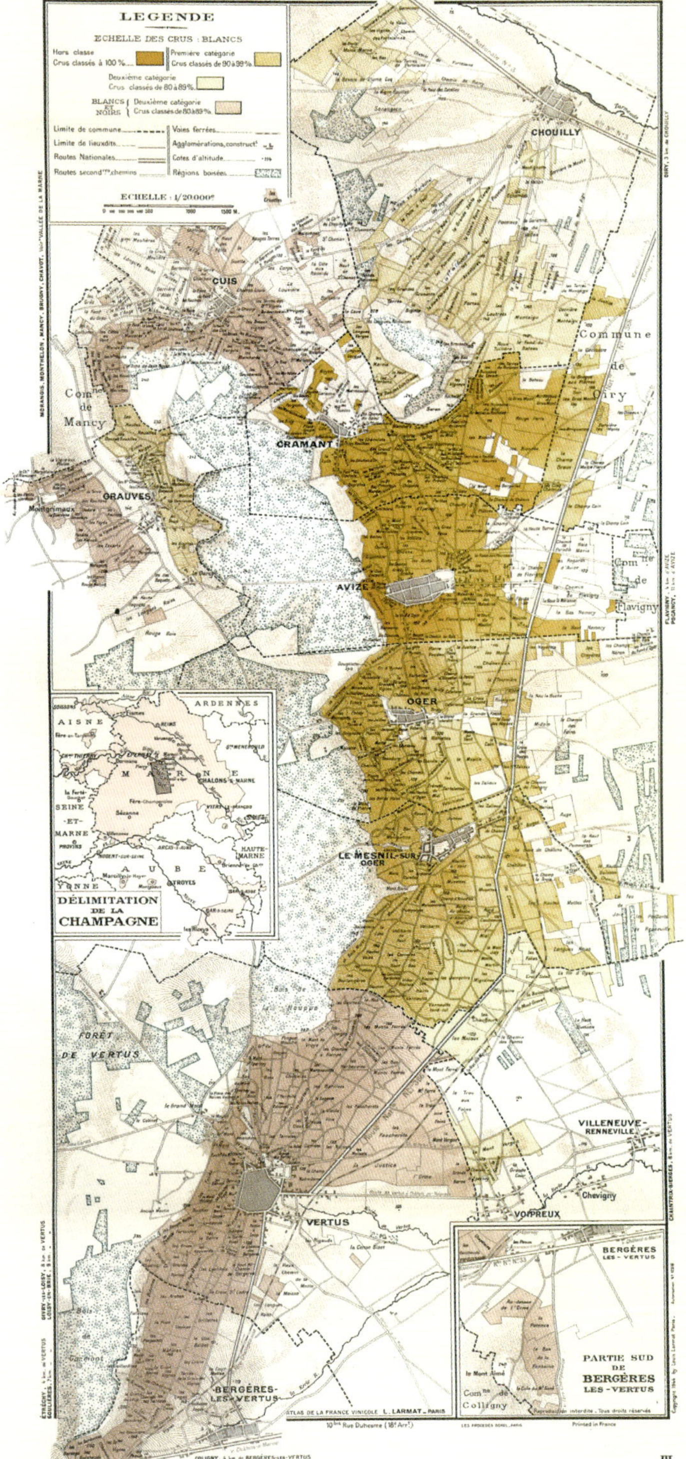

CÔTE DES BLANCS

As the name suggests, the region's white grape, chardonnay, dominates: four-fifths of these slopes south of Épernay are planted with it. Towards the top of the steepest vineyards in the Grand Cru village of Cramant, the chalk breaks through the topsoil to help produce wines of a searing, bone-dry, mineral intensity that can sometimes age for decades. Cramant's neighbours to the south – Avize, Oger and Le Mesnil-sur-Oger – and Chouilly to the north, are also all Grand Cru. While the Premier Cru village of Vertus, at the southern end of the Côte des Blancs, represents a lone outpost of fine pinot noir.

VALLÉE DE LA MARNE

The third key area stretches downstream along the Marne, producing wines once known as *vins de la rivière*. It begins with Aÿ, just east of Épernay, which vies with Sillery as the most historic name in the whole of Champagne. In the fifteenth century, Francis I declared he was king of Aÿ, and not just king of France, while Pope Leo the Magnificent would drink little else but the wines from this famous village. With its majestic Grand Cru vineyards sloping down to the Marne, Aÿ is home to some of the greatest pinot noir in the region and such esteemed Houses as Ayala, Bollinger and Deutz.

Around Épernay are Dizzy, Hautvilliers and Cumières, before you progress along the valley to the village of Château-Thierry and the western edges of Champagne. The chalk, so close to the topsoil around Aÿ, slips deeper underground as you move west, and the quality also decreases slightly, particularly on the north-facing slopes of the left bank. Some excellent pinot meunier is produced nonetheless, and this grape accounts for almost two-thirds of plantings in the Vallée de la Marne.

CÔTE DE SÉZANNE AND THE CÔTE DES BAR

The Côte de Sézanne is really a continuation of the Côte des Blancs, separated by the Saint Gond marshes, and with a similar preference for chardonnay, which makes up two-thirds of plantings. The wines are not as prestigious, however, and most find their way into non-vintage blends. Much larger in area is the Aube, or Côte des Bar as it is now called, which was once given over to gamay, and is now almost 90% pinot noir. With so little to spare from the Montaigne de Reims, particularly the Grand Cru and Premier Cru vineyards, this is *the* place every well-known Champagne House comes to source its pinot noir. As well as some of the prettiest countryside in Champagne, the Aube also boasts one of the hottest new areas for top-quality chardonnay planted on pure chalk on the slopes of the Montgueux hill, west of Troyes.

Left: A detailed map of the famous villages of the Côte des Blancs and its mix of Grand Crus and Premier Crus vineyards.

Opposite (top): Vineyard in autumn, Vallee de la Marne, Marne, Champagne-Ardenne, France.

Opposite (bottom): These painted, half-timbered houses, dating from the sixteenth century, are a feature of the ancient town of Troyes that, unlike Reims, survived the First World War intact. It is the capital of the Aube, or Côte des Bars as it's known in champagne circles.

TERROIR

It is a good two-hour drive to cross the champagne region from west to east or north to south, which allows for plenty of variation in all the factors that make up that gloriously French, catch-all word 'terroir'. The word evokes such natural, God-given variables as rainfall, elevation, soil and sunlight.

As in other wine regions, the best vineyards are on the slopes, usually halfway up and facing east or south-east to soak up as much early-morning sunshine as possible. There is a maritime influence in the heart of Champagne around Reims and Épernay and this helps to moderate the climate. That influence fades as you head south towards the Aube, where the climate has a more continental feel.

And yet there is no escaping the human factor in all this. In the vineyard the grower will decide which clone of which grape to plant and on which rootstock. He or she will also determine the density of vines per hectare, what training system to use, how to prune, what to spray and, crucially, when to harvest. In the cellar the balance tips firmly away from nature in favour of man. In his *World Encyclopedia of Champagne & Sparkling Wine*, Tom Stevenson compares champagne with port and sherry, and writes:

"It is impossible to produce such wines with a hands-off approach. They are the result of human meddling, intervention and sophistication and, of all these wines, champagne is perhaps the most technical, most demanding and most man-made." The ethos of the Champagne Houses, especially for their flagship, non-vintage expressions, is to produce something that never varies from one year to the next.

The vagaries of climate and, to some extent the essence of terroir itself, are blended away with grapes sourced from all four corners of Champagne and by using reserve wines from previous vintages to create a consistent House style. Like the big brands of Scotch whisky, the secret is all in the blend.

The component parts, whether from a particular distillery or vineyard, are like instruments in an orchestra whereby the whole is greater than the sum of its parts, or so people claim. But as in Scotland, this theory is

being challenged. Today there are a swathe of expensive, single-vineyard champagnes like Krug's Clos du Mesnil and Philipponnat's pioneering Clos des Goisses that first appeared in 1935. There are also many more grower champagnes keen to express the uniqueness of their vineyards, as a point of difference to the *négociants'* blends.

Champagne's original 'terroir-ist' was René Lamarre, author of *La Révolution champenoise*. In the late nineteenth century, he railed against the brand-owners as explained in the following passage from Kolleen Guy's fascinating book, *When Champagne Became French*: "By monopolizing production and promoting brand names through the Syndicat du Commerce, Lamarre argued, the négociants severed the wine from the heart and soul of Champagne, unjustly accruing all of the regional riches in the process. Terroir was being sacrificed to greed."

Zoom out of Champagne and you will discover it straddles latitude 49° north, the same as Quebec and Vancouver. This is on the cusp of where you can make wine in the northern hemisphere, and occasionally beyond – as it was during the mini ice age in the late seventeenth century. Today this limit is being edged northwards with annual temperatures rising by 1.3°C in the 30 years to 2020, although what really matters is the temperature during the growing season. In a good year the vines will have escaped any risk of a late frost to ripen gradually after flowering, traditionally for 100 days before the harvest. The aim is to pick grapes that are fully mature yet retain the acidity vital for any quality sparkling wine.

Today the average growing season has shortened to 87 days, and this was down to just 80 in the scorching hot summer of 2003, the first year that grapes were picked as early as August. For now, Champagne might be benefitting from rising temperatures, with well-ripened grapes that need little if any added sugar in the form of chaptalization (see p.20). However, climatic extremes are becoming more common, and new pests and diseases are appearing in the vineyards. If it keeps getting warmer, it might favour producers in England, although the climate is different and more maritime across the Channel.

CHALK

It is hard to exaggerate the importance of chalky soils in Champagne. Being so porous, chalk acts as a superb subterranean reservoir for the vines, holding up to 400 litres of water per cubic metre, while offering good drainage so the roots don't become waterlogged. It also acts as a solar panel to reflect sunlight and warmth onto the vine, and it adds a mineral precision to the wines, particularly chardonnay. In addition, its relative abundance attracted the Romans to mine the stuff and produce quicklime and whitewash for their buildings. By extending the mineshafts, the Champenois created the labyrinthine network of tunnels, or *crayères*, which have proved the perfect environment for a slow secondary fermentation in the bottle.

Of the various strains of chalk, the best is said to be belemnite from the remains of extinct sea creatures; this whole region was beneath the ocean until some 70 million years ago. The strata of chalk were pushed up by subsequent volcanic activity, and occasionally break through the surface. These chalky outcrops are known as the *Falaises de Champagne* and are most evident in prime sites on the Côte des Blancs and Montaigne de Reims. There are less porous types of chalk and a whole range of other soils including clay, marl, limestone and sandstone. Marl, for example, is richer in nutrients but doesn't drain so well, which can lead to fungal diseases in damp years.

Opposite: The water, a canal beside the River Marne, helps stabilise the climate of the steep, south-facing slopes of Philipponnat's fabled Clos des Goisses vineyards in Mareuil-sur-Aÿ.

Above (left): Part of Champagne Taittinger's 250-hectare estate; note how the rows of vines are angled to make best use of the sun's rays.

Above (right): Pure belemnite chalk in the Côte des Blancs, which lends great mineral precision to the chardonnay grown here.

THE CHAMPAGNE GRAPES

Having set the scene, it is time to introduce the cast. Over the centuries the number of grape varieties in champagne have been whittled down to just three, with the last main contender, gamay, banished from the aube in the 1960s. The three are: pinot noir, chardonnay and pinot meunier.

However, the choice of what variety to plant in which vineyard is greater than you might think if you consider there are more than 50 approved clones available, each with subtly different attributes. Pinot noir and chardonnay are the classic grapes of Burgundy, and it took a fair few centuries for the region's producers to finally concede they would never beat their southern neighbours when it came to still wines. Today, almost the sole survivors in Champagne of this ancient tradition of still wines are both made of pinot noir. From near Épernay, there is a tiny production of the delightfully named Bouzy Rouge from the eponymous village, pronounced 'boozy'. While from the Aube you can find the pink Rosé des Riceys.

As for the whites, one imagines the Burgundians were never remotely fazed by the still chardonnays once produced in Champagne. Here, in its raw state as *vin clair*, it seems skeletal with almost no flesh at all, and appears to contain enough acid to strip the enamel from your teeth. In this chilly, marginal climate, this is a variety that craves that little extra boost of alcohol and the gush of bubbles from a secondary fermentation. Within Champagne, 28.5% of the vineyards are planted with chardonnay. It is held in high esteem for its crisp elegance and finesse, particularly in its heartland of the Côte des Blancs. For blends it adds a racy backbone and freshness, while on its own as a Blanc de Blancs it can outlive any other style of champagne thanks to its acidity. With the very finest vintage cuvées, this recedes after a decade or two to reveal a toasty, almost Burgundian richness. Needless to say, even those who profess to hate chardonnay, guzzle it with glee.

By a small margin, pinot noir is the most planted grape in Champagne, accounting for 38.4% of the vineyards. The core area is the Montaigne de Reims, though it doesn't dominate to the same extent as chardonnay on the Côte des Blancs. It also soaks up the sunshine on the south-facing slopes of the right bank of the Marne, and accounts for four-fifths of plantings in the Côte des Bars – the prime source of pinot noir for standard non-vintage blends. Since the days of Dom Pérignon, this grape has been very gently crushed to avoid the clear-run juice being tinted by the skins.

Marginally less 'noble' is the third grape, pinot meunier, which covers 32.8% of Champagne's vineyards at present. Being a relatively late-budding variety, and thus less prone to late frosts, it is widely planted on the cooler, north-facing slopes of the Marne valley. Here it has been losing ground to pinot noir, with its vineyards down 7% since the 1980s according to the champagne expert, Michael Edwards. "This appears, at least in some cases, to have been driven by fashion and marketing, rather than by any serious concern to improve quality," he wrote in *The Finest Wines of Champagne*.

Aside from these three, a few other grapes are permitted, including petit meslier and arbane, along with a new variety called voltis, but the quantities are tiny. The vineyards are densely planted with 8–10,000 vines per hectare to ensure a healthy competition between them as their roots stretch out in search of water and nutrients from the soil. A month after the harvest, once the weather has turned cold, growers descend on their vineyards armed with pruning shears. The idea is to encourage each vine to concentrate its energies on a selected number of fruit-bearing buds and to stop them becoming too leafy. Proud of their pruning prowess, the growers aim to achieve the right balance of foliage to bunches of grapes, of which there should be 12–15, enough to produce one bottle per vine.

Under the rules of champagne, the grapes are all picked by hand because machine harvesting might damage the bunches and risk skin contact with the juice. The grapes are then quickly crushed as whole bunches, and separated into the cuvée, with the first three gentle presses, and the *tailles*, or tails, which are squeezed that much harder. In a bid to improve quality the Comité Interprofessionnel du vin de Champagne (CIVC) reduced the amount producers could extract from the *taille* by around a fifth in 1992.

Each pressing is kept separate to allow the winemaker more scope in constructing the particular blend. Multiply the number of pressings from a single plot by the number of vineyards, the range of grapes and different vintages, and you have an almost infinite spectrum of base wines to choose from. That said, the difference between these component parts tends to be very subtle since the base wine is, almost by definition, relatively neutral, low in alcohol and high in acidity.

From whatever cards nature has dealt, the winemaker, or *chef de cave*, has to try and shuffle them into a consistent House style, with a little help from the reserve wines of former years, unless making vintage champagne. This is no mean feat given the vagaries of the weather up here on the northern fringes of planet wine. Yet for the real artist in the cellar the cult of consistency must grate at times. Occasionally he or she will be invited to unleash their creative genius and construct something new, but it doesn't happen very often.

Opposite: The other component in the champagne mix is pinot meunier, these having just been picked in the Marne Valley, where it dominates the north-facing slopes.

Above (right): Chardonnay lends elegance and a racy acidity to all champagne blends that are not classified – Blanc de Noirs, and stars in its own solo performance as Blanc de Blancs.

Right: The other Burgundy grape, pinot noir, is the most planted variety in Champagne, accounting for just under 40% of the vines. It is also used to produce the region's still red wine – Bouzy Rouge.

HOW CHAMPAGNE IS MADE

The bubbles that define champagne have been part of winemaking for ever. They signify the start of fermentation after the grapes have been crushed and the end when the bubbling stops.

For the earliest winemakers this was the only visible sign that anything was actually happening. They couldn't see the few billion wild yeast cells attack the grape juice in a feeding frenzy until all the sugars had been converted to alcohol. What they were witnessing was the by-product of fermentation – carbon dioxide, which, if trapped in the bottle, will make any wine sparkle.

The story of sparkling wine has been a long slow evolution from accident to design. In an area like Champagne on the northern fringes of the wine world, it was always a challenge to complete fermentation before the cold weather put the yeast to sleep for the winter. Come the spring, the warm weather would rekindle the process causing the wine to fizz in cask or bottle. Local winemakers long considered this to be a curse until ironically it became the region's greatest virtue.

Secondary fermentation in a bottle evolved into a precise science and today the process is as follows: the champagne grapes of chardonnay, pinot noir and pinot meunier are harvested by hand and quickly pressed at the winery to separate the juice from the skins. Around four-fifths will be the cuvée, until the pressure in the presses is increased to extract the final *taille*, or tail. This might be sold off or blended back in to add structure to the wine.

The Champagne Houses buy in grapes from across the region and ferment them separately, as they do with the different grape varieties. Fermentation takes place in stainless-steel tanks, and sometimes in new or old oak barrels, occasionally with a little added sugar in cool years – a perfectly legal process known as chaptalization. Once complete, the cellars will be full of separate tanks of fairly neutral, acidic base wine with a strength of around 11.5%. There will be subtle differences between them, however, and this gives the winemaker the means to construct the House style. The blend, or *assemblage*, is created from January to March and involves blending in reserve wines from previous years in the case of non-vintage champagnes, which account for the vast majority of bottles drunk. They are easy to spot with their 'NV' on the label.

Vintage champagne with 100% of the grapes from a specific year, or a *cru* from a particular vineyard, will seek to express the vagaries of climate or terroir, while the dominant NV style is all about consistency. Either way, constructing the blend is almost certainly the most skilful part of the whole process. Once finished, the wine will be racked into

a clean tank and injected with the *liqueur de tirage* – a mix of sugar, champagne yeasts and some nutrients before bottling under a crown cap, like a beer bottle. The amount of sugar and yeast is carefully calibrated to achieve a precise pressure of up to 7 bar, akin to the tyre pressure of a double-decker bus.

The bottles are stacked horizontally in the cold, dank cellars of Champagne, and left to get on with it. The cellars form mile upon mile of tunnels hacked into the soft chalk, deep underground where the temperature remains a constant 10–12°C throughout the year. The yeasts have been specially cultured to cope with the chill and work under pressure as they feed on the sugar to boost the strength by a degree and create all those wonderful bubbles. The process can take up to three months, until all the yeast cells expire and sink to the bottom as lees. It is assumed they die happy, but their role is not over.

All champagne must be bottle-aged for a minimum of 15 months, of which at least a year will be on the lees. The dead cells start to break down in a slow process known as autolysis, which can last up to three or four years in the case of a prestigious vintage cuvée. Most champagnes are not given time for the full effects to appear, but this is where those subtle, nutty, toasty, brioche-like aromas come from.

The need to get shot of the lees in the bottle without losing the fizz was a conundrum the Champenois finally solved, through a process known as *remuage*. Traditionally this was done with a *pupitre*, which resembles a hefty, wooden sandwich board drilled with champagne-sized holes. Bottles were inserted at 45 degrees and gradually tilted each day with a vigorous shake of the wrist until all the yeasty sediment was down in the neck of the bottle. This riddling of the bottles by hand takes four to five weeks. As well as being extremely labour-intensive it probably caused a certain amount of repetitive strain injury. If you visit a Champagne House, or any producer of traditional sparkling wine, you will see rows of *pupitres* proudly displayed in the cellars. Behind the scenes, a rather more hi-tech if less glamorous solution has been found – the *gyropallette*, where a computerized machine can riddle a whole pallet of bottles in three to four days.

The next step is *dégorgement* where the neck of the upturned bottle is frozen, usually in liquid nitrogen, and the crown cap removed. The icy plug of yeast, about an inch long, shoots out like a champagne cork thanks to the pressure. The bottle is immediately topped up with a mix of the same wine and sugar syrup known as the *liqueur d'expédition* and corked before too many bubbles escape.

Opposite (top): Freshly picked chardonnay in a traditional 'Coquard' press found in many Champagne Houses. The key is to press the grapes as quickly as possible before the juice begins to oxidise.

Opposite (bottom): The time-honoured practice of riddling bottles in *pupitres* in the cellar. The technique, invented by Veuve Clicquot's *chef de cave* in the early nineteenth century, aims to jiggle the yeasty sediment into the neck of the bottle.

Above: Most champagne producers now use stainless steel tanks for fermentation rather than traditional oak barrels. This ensures that no extraneous aromatic components get conveyed and allows for a more pure wine.

VINTAGES AND STYLES

The last act of manipulation before the cork is rammed home, is the dosage – or quantity of sugar contained within the *liqueur d'expédition*. The sugar level starts from less than 2g/litre of sugar and goes up to more than 50g/l.

For those who like their fizz drier than the driest Martini with no added sugar, there is **Brut Nature** – also known as Non-Dosé, Ultra Brut, Brut Sauvage or, for the skinniest supermodel, Brut Zéro. Technically it can have up to 2g/litre of sugar, not that you would notice. It became trendy in the 1980s with the launch of Laurent-Perrier's Ultra Brut, which inspired other Houses to follow suit. While the style excited a number of sommeliers, sales were tiny. The trend seems to be fading now, not least because the wines often tasted hollow and unbalanced.

Next up is the merely searingly dry **Extra Brut**, where up to 6g/ litre of sugar are allowed. If the wine is really well made, such a low *dosage* can work. Then comes **Brut**, where the maximum sugar content is increased to 12g/litre. Given that the word translates as 'raw', and that it was off the scale of dryness for most champagne drinkers a century ago, certainly outside London, it has come a long way. Today even those sweet-toothed Russians have succumbed to the raw charms of Brut, which today accounts for over 95% of all champagne sold.

Beyond 12 grams you get to **Extra-Sec** or **Extra-Dry**. It has all but disappeared thanks to the global domination of Brut and a certain snobbish contempt for anything not bone-dry. Above 17 grams you are in the territory of **Sec** or **Dry**, before you hit **Demi-Sec** (33–50g/l) and finally **Doux** at over 50g/l. The terminology appears terribly dated since so-called 'dry champagne' would definitely be sweet by today's standards.

The evolution of sweetness is evident from Louis Roederer's Carte Blanche that boasted a sumptuous 180g/l of sugar in the early twentieth century. By the 1980s that had been cut by two- thirds, and today the wine contains 45g/l, putting it on the sweet side of Demi-Sec. Meanwhile within *Brut* there has been a shift to drier styles according to the *Drinks Business* editor Patrick Schmitt. When he researched the subject for his Master of Wine dissertation, he discovered that average dosage levels had fallen by 25% in the last 20 years, with most producers citing the 2003 heat wave as the turning point. So, is it all due to climate change?

Not according to Schmitt, who believes the main reason is down to the winemakers pursuing a drier style, which they prefer and believe their customers do too. Apparently this is backed up by a detailed study carried out by Moët & Chandon a few years ago. Whether consumer tastes have really become drier is a moot point, especially when you consider the success of Extra-Dry Prosecco.

Above: Led by Houses like Pommery, the first Brut champagnes began to gain popularity in England in the 1870s. Some went further, like the Laurent-Perrier *sans-sucre* or *Zéro Dosage* wine, released a decade later.

More than 80% of champagne is **non-vintage** and designated NV on the label. The amount of previous vintages included in the blend varies depending on the House style. A fresh, lively wine like Taittinger NV might contain barely one-tenth of a previous year, while something with the richness of Krug can stretch back over multiple vintages, with only half coming from the most recent one. Other NV champagnes might be entirely from a single year. They are not designed to improve with age on release, but that's not to say they won't if the quality is there and provided the bottles are stored somewhere cool and dark at a reasonably constant temperature of 10–15°C. Beyond a year or two, any improvements will be negligible until eventually the freshness starts to fade.

Vintage champagne does improve over time, especially if its producer gave it a good three or four years resting on its lees in the cellar before being disgorged. If you love those toasty, brioche-like aromas and flavours of fine vintage fizz, you should resist drinking the wine until a decade or so after the harvest. Such bottles imply the growing season was especially good, although not all producers are as discerning as others, and some will release a vintage almost every year.

The category has come under pressure from the top layer of champagnes, known as **prestige cuvées**. Sourcing the greatest vintages from the best vineyards available, the *chef de cave* of every Grand Marque will endeavour to blend the finest expression possible. The target audience demands nothing less and has the means to pay – although the market has shifted somewhat from those Russian Czars sipping Louis Roederer in lead crystal bottles at the Imperial Court. While some Houses focus all the high-end efforts on prestige cuvées, those that have persisted with vintage champagne are beginning to look relatively good value.

Champagne is invariably a blend of grapes, unless it is a pure chardonnay **Blanc de Blancs**. With its crisp, whip-clean effervescence and lemony freshness, this is often the lightest and most elegant style. By contrast, **Blanc de Noirs**, made from just black grapes, usually have a riper texture, with aromas of baked apple and spice, for example. You might find a deeper, more golden hue in a Blanc de Noirs, but no tinge of pink. For that there is **rosé champagne**, which is usually made from blending in a little red wine. All still rosé in Europe, from Puglia to Provence, is made by letting the colour from the skins bleed into the juice before it is run off. Simply marrying red and white wine is what the Californians do to make their sweet, bubblegum-pink blush wine, yet it seems to work in Champagne, often beautifully. And, though some Champenois prefer the skin contact method, it can be difficult to control the tannins.

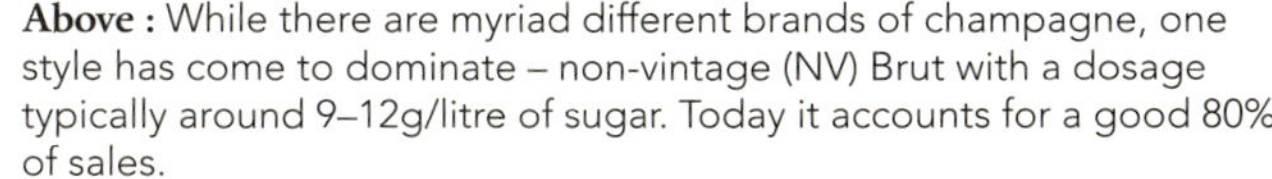

Above : While there are myriad different brands of champagne, one style has come to dominate – non-vintage (NV) Brut with a dosage typically around 9–12g/litre of sugar. Today it accounts for a good 80% of sales.

Right: Rosé once dismissed by many in the industry as being not altogether serious, has become one of the most exciting and dynamic categories of champagne.

SERVING, STORING AND BIBLICAL BOTTLES

Once upon a time going down to the cellar to fetch a bottle of champagne was a game of Russian roulette. The slightest flaw in the glass could turn any bottle into a lethal weapon.

One can imagine his Lordship in his drawing room startled by a muffled commotion from the bowels of his house, followed by the deep groan of an injured butler. Mercifully such accidents were abolished with the invention of strong, flawless glass in the nineteenth century.

Stronger bottles encouraged producers to ramp up the pressure to between 5 and 6 atmospheres at room temperature. If you were foolish enough to open champagne that warm, the cork would shoot out like a bullet, foam would spurt everywhere and what was left of the wine would go flat fairly fast. Unless you are a Formula One racing driver intent on spraying the crowds from the podium, this is best avoided.

However if the bottle is chilled down to 5°C, the pressure drops to 2.5 atmospheres, though you should still take care to point it away from anyone and hold your thumb over the cork as you free it from its wire cage. Then twist the bottle and let the cork ease itself out with no gush of foam. It sounds obvious, but accidents do happen. As retold in Don Hewitson's *Glory of Champagne*, *The Evening Standard* reported a doctor from Moorfield Eye Hospital saying: "We get at least two victims of champagne corks a week and often have to operate." Today it might well be a prosecco cork.

Alternatively, you may wish to unleash your inner Cossack, and slice open the bottle with a sabre. The rules of *sabrage*, as it is known, are as follows: make sure the bottle is well chilled and dry so it doesn't slip, and then take off the wire, strip off the foil and hold the bottle by the base, angled upwards. Make sure your thumb is tucked out of harm's way inside the punt, and that no one is in your line of fire. Then run the blade up the seam in the glass along the side of the bottle in a firm, gentle sweep. As you hit the glass collar on the neck it will fly off with a crack, taking the cork with it. Thanks to all that pressure in the bottle, it is easier than it looks. And you don't need a sabre – a big kitchen knife works just as well.

Champagne should be served at a chilly 5–9°C because it will warm up in the glass, but over-chilling a bottle, as can happen with ice buckets in a restaurant, will blunt the aromas and flavours. As for the glass, fashions have swung from the *coupe* to the flute to the tulip-shaped wine glass. The *coupe*, or saucer, is the oldest, in fact even older than its supposed inspiration – Marie Antoinette's left breast. There are tales of how the teenage queen would dress up as a milkmaid at her summer palace of Rambouillet, and that the king commissioned a *bol sein*, or breast bowl, for her dairy. In truth the champagne coupe was an Anglo-Italian invention of the 1660s from Venetian glassblowers employed by the Duke of Buckingham in London. Yet it was too good a myth to die, and supermodels Claudia Schiffer and Kate Moss have both bared their breasts for a modern version.

Above: Louis Roederer's *chef de cave* Jean-Baptiste Lécaillon inspecting one of his bottles by candle light in the cellars in Reims.

A pyramid of champagne saucers filled with fizz has a certain cheesy glamour, and the world record set in a Dutch shopping mall contained some 40,000 glasses, 63 storeys high. Yet the coupe has been banished to the cocktail bar thanks to its Babycham image and because the *mousse* of bubbles that took so long to create dissipate far too quickly. Champagne flutes are a lot better, though they are often too small and overfilled so you cannot properly appreciate the wine's aromas. As a result, a standard, tulip-shaped white wine glass is now favoured. Then again, you will get through more bottles than with flutes, which might be a consideration if you are paying for the party. And as for missing out on the bouquet you wonder how many guests would actually notice. Personally, I have never seen anyone swirl and sniff a glass of champagne at a wedding.

Another myth worth busting is that of the teaspoon dangled in an open bottle to preserve the sparkle. Various tests, including one by the CIVC, have shown it has no effect whatsoever. Much better is to invest in a champagne stopper with hinged sides that clip on to the bottle. So long as you keep it in the fridge you can extend the life of an opened bottle over a long weekend and have a delicious apéritif every evening. And it goes without saying that every fridge should hold a bottle of champagne ready for a spontaneous celebration.

The rules on storage are the same with any wine – somewhere dark where the temperature is cool and constant. Champagne seems particularly sensitive to UV light, which explains the use of dark green glass or a cellophane wrapper in the case of Louis Roederer. When it comes to buying champagne, so long as the bottle hasn't sat too long under shop lights, you should be fine.

BIBLICAL BOTTLES

Champagne comes in many sizes, from those often disappointing quarter-sized 'piccolo' bottles served on airlines, to those of truly biblical proportions.

MAGNUM
Two bottles (1.5l). Latin for 'great', and considered ideal for ageing vintage champagne.

JEROBOAM
Four bottles (3l). Named after the tenth-century king of northern Israel, and meaning 'he increases the people'.

REHOBOAM
Six bottles (4.5l). The son of Solomon, whose name means 'he who enlarges the people'.

METHUSELAH
Eight bottles (6l). Symbolic of great age, and named after an Old Testament patriarch who lived for 969 years.

SALMANAZAR
12 bottles (9l). Named after the Assyrian king Shalmaneser.

BALTHAZAR
16 bottles (12l). Named after the king of Arabia who presented gifts to the baby Jesus.

NEBUCHADNEZZAR
20 bottles (15l). Named after the most powerful of all Babylonian kings, who ruled from the late seventh to the middle sixth century BCE.
Beyond lies the Solomon at 24 bottles and the Sovereign at 35 bottles, according to Taittinger, possibly the only producer. For one bottle more there is the Primat, and finally the Melchizedek, or Midas, which boasts the equivalent of 40 bottles. For one sprayed in gold paint from Armand de Brignac (Ace of Spades), a brand that is co-owned by the rapper Jay Z, expect to pay around £60,000.

VERTUS
PIERRY
BAYE
ETOGES

2

THE HISTORY OF CHAMPAGNE

Champagne has been at the crossroads of war and trade since Attila the Hun paid an unwelcome visit in the fifth century. The region's wines are just as old, but the transition from still to sparkling is far more recent and might not have happened without the English.

STARS IN THEIR EYES

The world's most famous wine was not invented per se, it was the product of a gradual evolution. Yet this did not stop the industry from later claiming that one man from the middle years of the last millennium, was the founding father of champagne.

"Come quickly. I'm drinking the stars!" cried the blind Benedictine monk, Dom Pérignon, having just created the most famous wine in the world. His moment of ecstasy was captured in stone in a life-size statue of him holding a foaming bottle of champagne. It stands on a plinth in the grounds of Moët & Chandon in Épernay in the heart of the Champagne region, and was used into the 1950s to advertise the Dom Pérignon brand. By 2007 that image had long gone, to be replaced by Claudia Schiffer, splayed across an unmade bed clutching a magnum-sized bottle, wearing fishnet tights, come-to-bed eyes and little else.

Quite what Dom Pérignon would have made of the German supermodel is anyone's guess, but one thing's for sure – the idea he invented sparkling champagne is pure fantasy. He wasn't even blind, and as for "drinking the stars", the only reference to that came 200 years later in a print advert from the late nineteenth century. Yet he was certainly involved in the region's wines and did much to improve their quality as cellar master at the Abbaye Saint-Pierre d'Hautvillers, just north of Épernay. It was one of his successors, Dom Grossard, who first propagated the myth about champagne in the 1820s.

Pérignon took up the post in 1668, aged 30, and remained there until his death in 1715. The crucial point to understand is that he and his fellow local winemakers produced champagne as a still wine. The presence of fizz in the finished product was proof that fermentation had not finished when it should have done. Bubbles were a fault to be stamped out, not least because they were dangerous. They were liable to shatter the relatively feeble bottles made of French glass, assuming any CO_2 hadn't already escaped through the *broquelet* – a primitive wooden stopper,

Above: The famous Abbaye Saint-Pierre d'Hautvillers, just north of Épernay, where Dom Pérignon was cellar master until 1715. It was bought by Comte Pierre-Gabriel Chandon with its surrounding vineyards a century later.

Opposite (left): The star-struck monk Dom Pérignon having just invented sparkling champagne, or so the story goes. A life-size statue of him stands in the grounds of Moët & Chandon's headquarters in Épernay.

Opposite (right): Charles X was the last French monarch to be crowned in the Cathedral of Notre-Dame de Reims, (Our Lady of Reims) in 1825, bringing to an end a tradition that had lasted since the First Millennium.

dipped in oil and wrapped in hemp. Until the Champenois readopted that old Roman invention – the cork – sparkling wine was best avoided.

During his time at Hautvillers, Pérignon doubled the Abbey's vineyards to 20 hectares and focused on pinot noir among the various varieties grown in the region. He believed this noble grape, responsible for the great reds of Burgundy, was less volatile than white varieties and therefore less likely to re-ferment in the bottle or cask. He insisted the vines should be vigorously pruned to no more than a metre in height, and that the harvest be done with the utmost care so the grapes didn't split. Wine derives its colour from the skins of the grapes and he wanted to make a white pinot noir. Because horses were liable to become overexcited, he recommended using mules or donkeys to transport the grapes safely, which should be quickly pressed to minimize skin contact. Once the colour started to bleed through in the fourth or fifth pressing, the wine was to be rejected. As his successors at the Abbey noted, he was quite the perfectionist.

Champagne's name comes from *Campania*, which the Romans called this region east of Paris presumably because it reminded them of the open, rolling countryside of Campania, south of Rome. They planted the first vines here, though the earliest recorded vineyard was that of Saint Rémy in the fifth century. He was famous because his baptism of Clovis, the king of the Franks in ad 496, began the country's conversion to Christianity. It happened in Reims, the cathedral city and regional hub that became the spiritual capital of France, like Canterbury in England. It was here that nearly all the French kings were crowned from Hugh Capet in 987 to Charles X in 1825, and this connection with royalty obviously boosted the reputation of the region and its wines. In the fifteenth century, not content with being just king of France, Francis I decreed that he was also *Roi d'Aÿ et de Gonesse* – Aÿ being a village east of Épernay whose vineyards were held in high regard and whose name was sometimes used to mean any wine from Champagne. The wines were otherwise referred to as *vins de Reims*, from the hillside of the so-called Montagne de Reims, or *vins de la rivière* from the Marne valley.

The River Marne flows west to join the Seine on the outskirts of Paris, which meant the wine could be shipped direct to the capital. In the other direction was the Rhineland, while to the north were the Low Countries and to the south, Switzerland. The Champagne region was thus strategically placed at a crossroads and there was a great deal of passing trade to be had. Unfortunately any merchant heading south would progress on to the warmer vineyards of Burgundy, where the red wines were undoubtedly better.

Winemakers in Champagne could manage only a pale imitation – deep pink at best and with a flavour that would have been quite acidic. As the climate cooled during the little ice age that began in the fifteenth century, the wines would have become even more tart. Some producers apparently added elderberries to boost the colour, though one wonders if many people were fooled. It seemed better to stick to making white wines, especially if you could vinify the clear juice of pinot noir without it being tinted by the skins, a trick supposedly pulled off by Dom Pérignon in Hautvillers.

Yet it was another Benedictine abbey, in the village St Hilaire in the foothills of, Limoux, southern France, that lays claim to the first recorded trade in sparkling wines as early as 1531. They had access to corks to keep the bubbles in what became known as Blanquette de Limoux. Despite its 160-year head start, the wine has been somewhat eclipsed by champagne.

AN ANGLO-FRENCH CREATION

Sparkling champagne as we know it today, owes a debt to a long-forgotten figure across the Channel – a man who had no links to the wine's homeland, but who understood the science behind the bubbles.

In England, champagne had its very own ambassador in the Marquis de St Evremond, who had been exiled to London in 1662. He was an aesthete and friend of Charles II, who as a joke made him warden of Duck Island in the pond in St James' Park and paid him an annual stipend of £300 – a fortune in those days. But Evremond was not a proponent of sparkling champagne. For him it was invariably a still wine, be it red from pinot noir grown on the slopes of the Montagne de Reims, or white from top villages like Hautvillers and Sillery.

So if it wasn't Dom Pérignon, who did put the fizz in champagne? Step forward Christopher Merret, an English physician and scientist born around 1615. He was a founding member of the Royal Society and had a particular interest in glass, which the English had been making in coal-fired furnaces since the early seventeenth century. They had been using wood as French glassmakers still did, but King James I had wanted to preserve the forests for shipbuilding. Using coal meant higher temperatures and therefore much stronger glass for making bottles. In those days wine was shipped in casks over to England, where it was bottled and stoppered with a cork. All things considered, sparkling wine was a much more viable proposition on the English side of the Channel.

In 1662 Merret delivered a paper to the Royal Society entitled 'Some Observations concerning the Ordering of Wines', which was unearthed by the wine writer Tom Stevenson fairly recently. It detailed the practice of adding sugar or molasses to a cask to make a wine taste 'brisk' and 'sparkling'. The yeast cells would emerge from their winter nap to feast on the sugar, burp CO_2 and die, though whether or not Merret understood this is unclear. But it was the first record of how to deliberately provoke a second fermentation and create a fizz, or mousse, in the wine. Indeed the first ever mention of sparkling champagne comes in a Restoration comedy, shortly afterwards, in 1676, *The Man of Mode* or *Sir Fopling Flutter*, by Sir George Etherege:

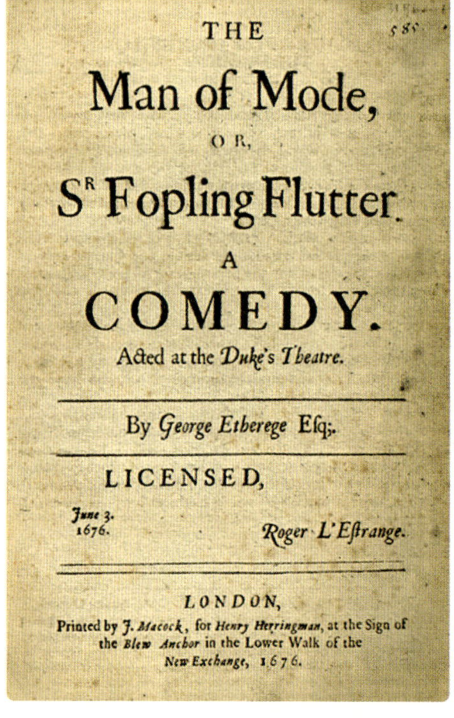

THE

Man of Mode,

OR,

S^R Fopling Flutter.

A

COMEDY.

Acted at the *Duke's Theatre.*

By *George Etherege* Esq;.

LICENSED,

June 3. 1676. *Roger L'Estrange.*

LONDON,

Printed by *J. Macock*, for *Henry Herringman*, at the Sign of the *Blew Anchor* in the Lower Walk of the *New Exchange*, 1676.

To the mall and the park
Where we love til 'tis dark,
Then sparkling champaign
Puts an end to their reign;
It quickly recovers
Poor languishing lovers,
Make us frolick and gay, and
drowns all our sorrows;
But, alas! We relapse again
on the morrow.

So it seems the English were the first to enjoy the wine and its frolicsome effect, but to say they invented it is probably a stretch. It was, after all, the Champenois who made the wine with its occasionally unfermented yeast, and to be honest it wasn't really an invention at all, more a very slow evolution that took a century and a half. Let us just say, in the spirit of the Entente Cordiale, that champagne was an Anglo-French creation, and that the world is all the better for it. But whatever the truth, back in the vineyards of Champagne it was certainly no overnight conversion from still wine to full-on fizz.

It was only in the third edition of the posthumous memoir about Dom Pérignon that a note was added claiming "a credible witness" had seen him lace his wines with a mixture of peaches, nuts and sugar candy to encourage the mousse. The poor monk would have been turning in his grave. As the French writer Raymond Dumay put it: "He knew of no enemy more dangerous than a wine which 'worked', that is to say a wine which, despite everything, was determined to bubble for the whole of its life." Sparkling champagne was considered the devil's wine for the way it could blow up in your face, or set off a chain reaction in the cellar and destroy hundreds of bottles. Nor was it considered a serious wine. "A wine will turn frothy particularly if it is strong and green ... froth is suitable only for chocolate, beer or whipped cream," wrote the wine merchant Bertin de Rocheret in 1726. Among connoisseurs, and most winemakers in Champagne, that view endured throughout the eighteenth century.

Yet among London's café society and the court of Versailles in France, the capricious nature of those bubbles must have enhanced the wine's appeal. There was something so haphazard and magical about the sparkle and whether it would happen at all. As the cork was eased from the bottle – would there be a deathly sigh or an exhilarating pop and rush of foam? Perhaps for some the risk of the bottle exploding like a grenade added an extra frisson of excitement.

In England, champagne had its very own ambassador in the Marquis de St Evremond, who had been exiled to London in 1662. He was an aesthete and friend of Charles II, who as a joke made him warden of Duck Island in the pond in St James' Park and paid him an annual stipend of £300 – a fortune in those days. But Evremond was not a proponent of sparkling champagne. For him it was invariably a still wine, be it red from pinot noir grown on the slopes of the Montagne de Reims, or white from top villages like Hautvillers and Sillery.

The Marquis de Sillery and his descendants owned a 50-hectare estate which they supplemented with other vineyards to create a blend and arguably the first real brand of champagne, though never a sparkling one. It was particularly prized in Britain, but to secure an allocation you needed contacts, which is where Evremond came in. Meanwhile, back in France, the still red wines of champagne had suffered a blow when King Louis XIV's doctor persuaded him in 1695 to switch to Burgundy for the sake of his health. For the next 50 years the Champenois fought a losing battle with the Burgundians over who could produce the best red wine from pinot noir.

Others saw it more as a rosé, or 'clairet', whose colour was often referred to as partridge eye or onion skin, while some winemakers favoured Dom Pérignon's approach of minimal skin contact for the clearest, palest wines. As for those occasional rogue bottles that sparkled, the first mention in France referred to a *mousse argentine*, or silvery fizz, in 1712. At the time it seemed most unlikely it would ever catch on.

Opposite (far left): Christopher Merret, an English physician and scientist, wrote the first paper on how to deliberately cause wines to sparkle with the addition of sugar.

Opposite (middle): The first ever mention of sparkling champagne appeared in this Restoration comedy by George Etherege, first performed in London in 1676.

Opposite (right): A noted bon viveur and wit, the Marquis de St Evremond was champagne's first unofficial ambassador in England, where he was exiled in 1662. For Evremond, however, champagne was invariably a still wine.

Above: Jean-François de Troy's *Le Déjeuner d'huîtres* (The Oyster Lunch, 1735) is believed to be the first time champagne bottles appeared in a painting. It could not have been a more glamorous debut.

FRIVOLOUS FIZZ

Sparkling champagne received a boost in France under the playful Philippe, Duke of Orléans, who succeeded the somewhat austere Louis XIV as regent in 1715. The French nobility took to this new vice during the regency, following in the footsteps of their kindred spirits in England.

On which note, it's impossible to know how many casks were being shipped to the b*on viveurs* Sir Fopling Flutter, and his ilk in London, and sweetened up to provoke a secondary fermentation, but there was certainly a tradition of doctoring wines. Port and sherry were invariably fortified to survive the rough crossing across the Bay of Biscay, by Britain's ex-pat wine trade in Porto and Jerez. According to Nicholas Faith in *The Story of Champagne*, only the wines of Burgundy and Champagne arrived here in their natural state. They didn't need fortifying for the 20-mile crossing over the Channel, though in the case of champagne it was best to bottle the wines quickly.

Winemakers in Champagne were soon in a better position to attempt to make sparkling wines if they wished to do so. A new glassworks was established in the nearby forest of Argonne to produce stronger bottles, and the use of cork stoppers, first introduced by the Romans, became widespread again. The law that theoretically banned the transport of bottled wine outside Champagne, except for the privileged few, was repealed in 1728. And seven years later, the quality and weight of the bottles was fixed by a royal decree which also stipulated that the cork should be tied on with a piece of string. In the meantime Nicolas Ruinart, a local wool merchant, established the first Champagne House in Épernay in 1729.

The balance of power in the region's wine trade was shifting. Reims, whose agents, or *courtiers*, had once enjoyed a monopoly, was losing out to Épernay, whose merchants began supplying European markets direct. In the mid-eighteenth century the strongest demand came from the Low Countries and the many German courts that slavishly followed the

Above: The amount of wine that was being shipped into England from France is clear in this satirical print from 1757, 'Humbly address'd to the laudable association of anti-gallicans'.

fashions of Versailles. After Ruinart, others began setting up shop. There was Claude Moët, a local vineyard owner who established his family firm in Épernay in 1743, and Florens-Louis Heidsieck, the first of the German merchants to arrive. His compatriots were to play a major role in the history of champagne in the nineteenth century.

Yet most producers remained sceptical of this frivolous new fad for fizz. Nicolas Bidet, born in 1709, a local author of various wine books, was convinced it was ruining the region's reputation as a source of good-quality still wines. You can almost hear the sneer in the following passage: "The vivacity, the exuberance of Champagne's wines, known in Paris only under the name of sparkling wine, this froth, this creamy mousse so dear to the heart of the ladies ... is responsible." There were various degrees of frothiness starting with the *tisane de champagne*, which barely bubbled at all, through *pétillant* to *demi-mousseux* that was similar to a *crémant* or *frizzante* style of prosecco. While sparkliest of all was the *saute-bouchon*, or 'cork jumper', though even this would have contained about half the pressure of today's bottles.

Whether or not it was worth ignoring Bidet's disdain, there was no consensus among producers where the bubbles came from. The white grapes grown on the chalky soils of the Côte des Blancs, south of Épernay, now almost exclusively planted with chardonnay, seemed especially prone to it. So too were wines that were particularly green and acidic. Some thought it was down to the temperature of the cellars where the bottles were kept, others blamed the cycles of the moon. But whatever the cause, there were sound, practical reasons for producers not to indulge the market for them. "At the beginning of the eighteenth century they were already aware of the more frequent accidents and the principal technical troubles found with sparkling wine," wrote Armand de Maizière in his book on the origins of the champagne trade, published in 1848. "... invariably some recalcitrant bottles did not sparkle at all ... [while others] exploded with a high-pitched crack enough to break their neighbours: explosive breakages in otherwise recalcitrant bottles; corks which proved defective either because of the cork itself, or because they were simply too small: wines which were sick because of thickness, grease, bitterness, acidity" ... and so on. It was clearly far safer to stick to the tranquillity of still wines, and hope the fashion for bubbles would soon pop.

Winemakers could expect to lose one-third to one-half of their bottles every year, according to one eighteenth-century figure in the trade. He believed such wastage bumped up the price of sparkling champagne to eight times its true value. Of course the high price only fuelled the desire among its well-heeled clientele, and this became a recurrent theme in the history of champagne and the creation of luxury brands. Being expensive and therefore exclusive was the perfect start for what became a liquid status symbol as the reason for the high price slowly shifted from the cost of production to the cost of marketing.

Deluxe brands were way in the distance, however, as the Ancien Régime began to crumble in the late eighteenth century. While the working-class *sans-culottes* in Paris were storming the Bastille in 1789, the peasant farmers of Champagne were complaining they lived on nothing but bread soaked in salt water. However much their fate improved after the French Revolution, the immediate beneficiaries were the merchants. As the old estates belonging to the monasteries or local families like the Marquis de Sillery were broken up into small parcels, the merchants' names evolved into brands.

Above (left): Nicolas Ruinart, founder of the oldest established Champagne House in 1729. He was apparently inspired by his uncle Dom Thierry Ruinart to believe there was a future for 'wine with bubbles'.

Above (right): Claude Moët was a grower and winemaker who was supplying the court at Versailles before setting up his own Champagne House in 1743.

CHAMPAGNE COMES OF AGE

France changed irrevocably on 14 July 1789, the day of the revolution. Yet it was a case of *plus ça change, plus c'est la même chose*, or business as usual, for the nascent champagne industry as it adapted to life under the new regime.

Sales of champagne doubled in the latter part of the eighteenth century, and stood at 288,000 bottles in the year before the Revolution in 1789. How much was sparkling is hard to say, but probably no more than one-tenth. It is also unclear how much was still being shipped in cask, whether to be drunk as a still wine or deliberately re-fermented into fizz with a few spoonfuls of sugar. Either way, by 1794, the Napoleonic Wars had pushed up the price of champagne to 90 shillings a case, double that of any other wine.

The Moët family certainly got off to a good start under the new regime when Jean-Rémy Moët was appointed mayor of Épernay in 1792. Seven years later a certain François-Marie Clicquot married Barbe-Nicole Ponsardin secretly in a cellar. According to legend, the priest gave the happy couple a book about Dom Pérignon. Clicquot's father was a local banker and tradesman who owned a vineyard near the delightfully named village of Bouzy, east of Épernay, and had a small winery there. Ponsardin was even better connected. Her father was a successful textile merchant turned Jacobin whom Napoleon made mayor of Reims.

In 1805 M. Clicquot died, leaving a three-year-old daughter, a business that involved banking, wool and champagne, and a 27-year-old widow. As Veuve Clicquot, Barbe-Nicole was to have a huge impact on champagne, and her own brand in particular. Given the contemporary mores about women staying at home, something the Napoleonic Code upheld, being a widow may have been her salvation. She realized they were the "only women granted the social freedom to run their own affairs". The champagne side of the business had been flourishing under her late husband, with sales up from 8,000 bottles in 1796 to 60,000 in 1804. But with the Royal Navy tightening its blockade as the war in Europe continued, the prospects looked grim.

Sales of Veuve Clicquot dropped to 10,000 bottles a year, and her erstwhile business partner, Alexandre Fourneaux, gave up. "Business terribly stagnant," wrote her head salesman, Louis Bohne, in 1810. "No sea traffic due to the English fleet. In Vienna the nobility has no money

to pay tradesmen not having sold any wheat for three years. Prices are plummeting." One assumes he was referring to sparkling champagne, which was still a very different drink to what we enjoy today. It tended to be cloudy and, although you could decant it into a new bottle you risked losing much of the sparkle. It was at least 10 times sweeter than a modern-style Brut champagne, and had none of those elegant little bubbles to tickle your nose. The bubbles were fat and gassy like those on a pint of beer, and Madame Clicquot called them 'toad's eyes'.

She set about perfecting the art of *remuage*, with her cellar master, Antoine-Aloys de Muller. He cut slanting holes in an old desk, or *pupitre*, into which the bottles were placed neck first for four months of riddling. With a daily quarter-turn and a quick jiggle, the lees eventually collected behind the cork. Keeping the bottle at an angle, the cork and sediment were fired into a bucket, the bottle flipped round, topped up with the sugary *liqueur de tirage*, and quickly recorked. Corks were originally inserted by the workers using their teeth, apparently, which must have kept the local dentists busy. In time producers progressed to using a hammer and then a corking machine in 1827.

"Spring water is not as clear," boasted Louis Bohne about the improved champagne, though Madame Clicquot failed to keep the method secret from her rivals. In 1811 a bright comet streaked across the skies above Champagne, heralding the best vintage anyone could recall. The Russians were developing a taste for fizz, only for the Czar to ban French wine imports in 1812. Scenting an opportunity, Bohne sailed for Königsberg on the Prussian coast and managed to pre-sell his consignment before reaching St Petersburg. "All their tongues are hanging out to taste it," he wrote of the famed 'Vin de la Comète', "and if it's as good as it is beautiful, they will all end up loving me."

Other merchants were eyeing up the Russian market. In 1812 Charles-Henri Heidsieck rode into Moscow on a white stallion ahead of Napoleon's advancing army with champagne to sell to the victor, whoever that might be. Two years later Russian and Prussian troops had swept into France and captured Reims. With Cossacks laying waste to the vineyards and plundering bottles of champagne, Madame Clicquot and others were frantically bricking up their cellars. It was around this time that the first cavalry officer sliced open a bottle with his sabre, in what became known as *sabrage*. Whether he was a Cossack or a dashing French hussar is unclear, but it certainly added to the glamour of champagne. During the protracted negotiations of the Congress of Vienna, which lasted from September 1814 through to the following June and the Battle of Waterloo, the wine was served at countless receptions and parties. Its bond with celebration and good times was being cemented.

While Veuve Clicquot and later Roederer secured their grip on Russia, which was soon the second biggest export market after Britain, new Champagne Houses were popping up in Épernay and Reims. Henriot opened in 1808, followed by Perrier-Jouët and Laurent-Perrier a few years later, then Mumm and Bollinger in the 1820s, and Pommery and others a decade later. The old Rue de Châlons in Épernay was fast becoming the grand Avenue de Champagne. By 1848, a book on the origins of champagne was claiming that: "Sparkling wines have made fortunes for twenty merchants [and] ensure an honest living for a hundred more." Champagne was coming of age.

Opposite: The Emperor Napoleon striking a classic pose in the cellars of his close friend Jean-Rémy Moët in July 1807. As well as running his champagne business, Moët was mayor of Épernay.

Below: The protracted negotiations of the Congress of Vienna (1814–15) were an attempt to redraw Europe's boundaries and achieve a lasting peace after the Napoleonic wars.

NAPOLEON TO THE *BELLE ÉPOQUE*

In the early 1800s Jean-Antoine Chaptal, a physician and Napoleon Bonaparte's interior minister, advocated sugar as a cure for green, unripe wines in France's cooler vineyard regions like Champagne.

Adding sugar boosts the alcoholic strength and amount of fizz in the case of sparkling wine, but the question was how much to add before the bottles exploded. This was resolved to a large extent by André François, a local chemist who devised a scientific formula in 1836.

Breakages were reduced to around 5%, and it allowed producers to safely increase the pressure in the bottle halfway towards the full-on fizz of today. Much more important, it made sparkling champagne a truly viable business for the first time. It attracted a growing crowd of commercially savvy producers. There were the Germans like Krug, Deutz, Mumm and Bollinger, and a number of entrepreneurial French Houses including Mercier and Pommery, both founded in 1858. This new generation of merchants wasted no time in carving out global markets and building their brands. Some of the original Champenois like the Comte de Villermot thought it vulgar to put one's name on a label, but that wasn't an issue for his son-in-law Jacques Bollinger.

By 1870 production had reached 20 million bottles from barely a million at the start of the century. Almost every inch of the Marne's traditional slopes was now carpeted with vines. Tastes varied within different markets, with the prize for the sweetest tooth going to Russia. According to the drinks journalist Patrick Schmitt MW: "There are stories of Russian Czars drinking it with 200 grams per litre of sugar which is more than a can of Coke." Roederer became the 'Official Supplier to the Imperial Court of Russia', for which it created the famous sweet cuvée Cristal in 1876.

Mainland Europe, including France, preferred their champagne considerably sweeter than today because it was served with the pudding or afterwards as a toast. In Britain it was drunk as an apéritif, since after-dinner drinking favoured sweet, fortified wines like Port and Madeira. Portuguese wines had enjoyed a tax advantage over French wines ever since the Methuen Treaty of 1703, which the British Chancellor, William Gladstone, corrected only in 1860. Champagne remained a drink to aspire to with prices to match, but it was increasingly within reach of the middle classes, and UK sales trebled over the next 30 years. By 1900 40% of the wine's entire production, or 10.75 million bottles, were consumed by the Brits, an amount not exceeded until the 1970s.

Opposite: A portrait of Tsar Nicholas II of Russia, raising a toast of his beloved champagne, published in *Vanity Fair*, 21 October 1897.

Left: Czar Nicholas II, the last Emperor of Russia, with his wife Alexandra, at a New Year's Day reception in 1897. The Russian court was awash with champagne, particularly the syrupy-sweet cuvées of Roederer and Veuve Clicquot.

Below: Mercier's giant barrel held the equivalent of 200,000 bottles of wine and weighed so much that two bridges collapsed on its journey to Paris in 1889.

Verre a champagne
par Ch. Chenavard

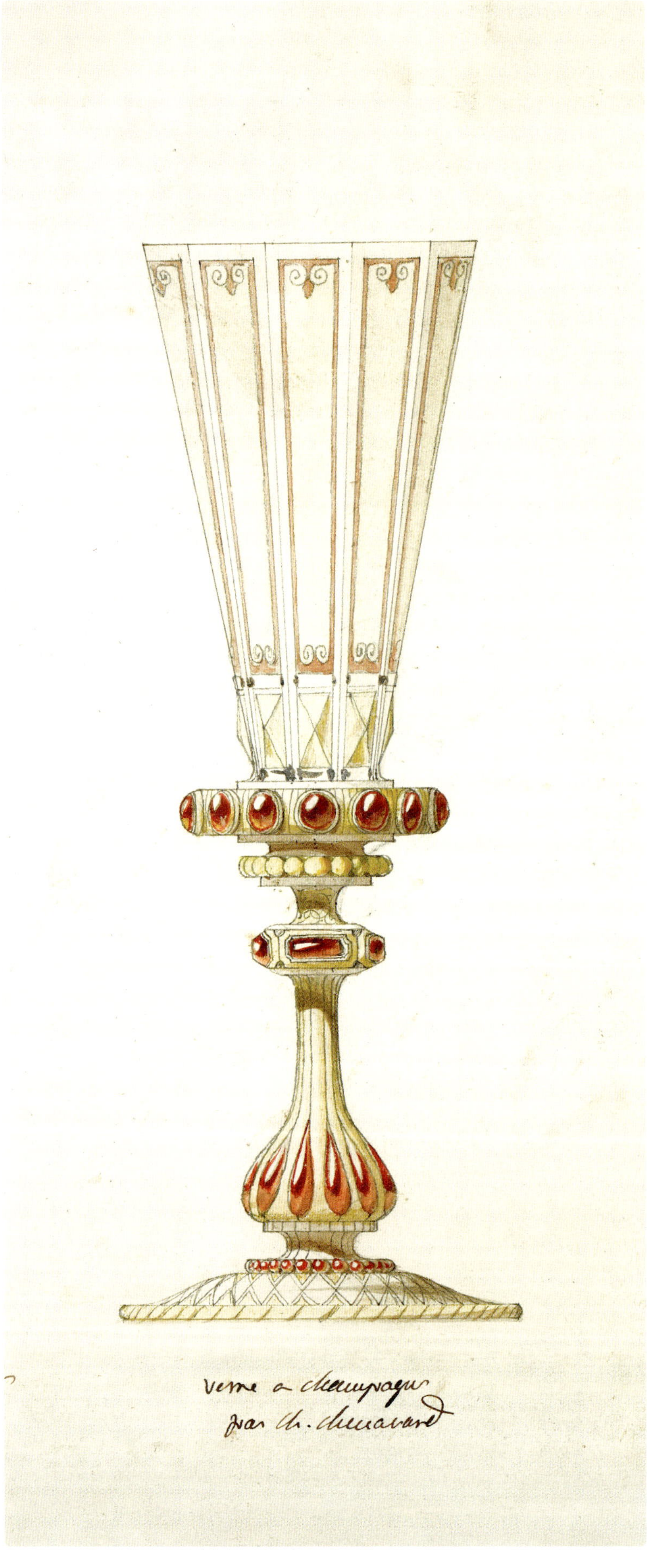

Verre a champagne
par Ch. Chenavard

Clicquot and Heidsieck were shipping wines to England labelled 'Dry' as early as 1857, followed by 'Very Dry' from Bollinger in 1868. Other terms like 'Extra Sec' or 'Extra Dry' were used as tastes for richer styles of champagne began to fade. Madame Pommery, an astute businesswoman and widow very much in the mould of Veuve Clicquot, launched the first Brut champagne in 1874, having opened a London office 13 years earlier. For decades Pommery was the UK's most popular champagne, though 'Brut' remained a minority interest for some time.

The devastating Franco-Prussian War of 1870 saw the vineyards overrun, Paris under siege and the end of Napoleon III's rule. When the Prussians withdrew, Champagne entered a golden age that was to last until 1914. After the horrors of the First World War, the era was given the rose-tinted title of the Belle Époque – a halcyon period of peace and prosperity when the arts and science flourished. This was the time of Toulouse-Lautrec, Maxim's and the Folies Bergère when the bourgeoisie embraced the fashions of Parisian high society, or 'Le Tout-Paris', and dined out on a rising tide of champagne. The drink's image was everywhere from posters in the Metro to adverts in magazines, all seeking to capture the essential *joie de vivre* in those bubbles. Sex was a recurrent theme. One brand featured a crusty old gent on all fours fumbling to attach a garter to the leg of a young woman, presumably his mistress. A free pair of garters was offered with every bottle.

As Paris prepared for the Universal Exhibition in 1889, with its 'temporary' metal entrance – the Eiffel Tower – Eugène Mercier had the world's biggest barrel filled with champagne and towed to the city by 24 white oxen. News of the stunt was reported as far afield as San Francisco. Paris, with its *fin de siècle* decadence and glamour, was more about image than sales for the big Champagne Houses whose sights were on burgeoning export markets like America. Charles Heidsieck, the original 'Champagne Charlie', first crossed the Atlantic back in 1852 and ended up being captured by Union troops in the American Civil War. Within a decade of the war's ending in 1865, US exports were approaching 400,000 bottles, led by Piper-Heidsieck. In 1876, Mumm released Cordon Rouge, which was an instant hit in France and easy to remember for visiting tourists due to its striking red sash across the label. Five years later it was launched in the States and spread fast through nightclubs, restaurants and brothels. It flowed through New Orleans jazz clubs and inspired the 'Cordon Rouge Gallop' – a prelude to rap music's embrace of Cognac a century later and the Busta Rhymes hit 'Pass the Courvoisier'. By 1903 the biggest brand in the States was Moët & Chandon's White Seal with sales of over 1.2 million bottles, a quarter of Moët's entire production.

Left: A trio of highly ornate champagne flutes from the 1830s.

Overleaf (left): The trademark registration by Chandon & Co. for their White Seal label, 1887.

Overleaf (right): "Gentlemen!! Do you wish to conquer hearts!" declares this saucy poster for a long forgotten brand. Somehow, it's clear the coquettish lady with the black tights and splayed legs is not his wife.

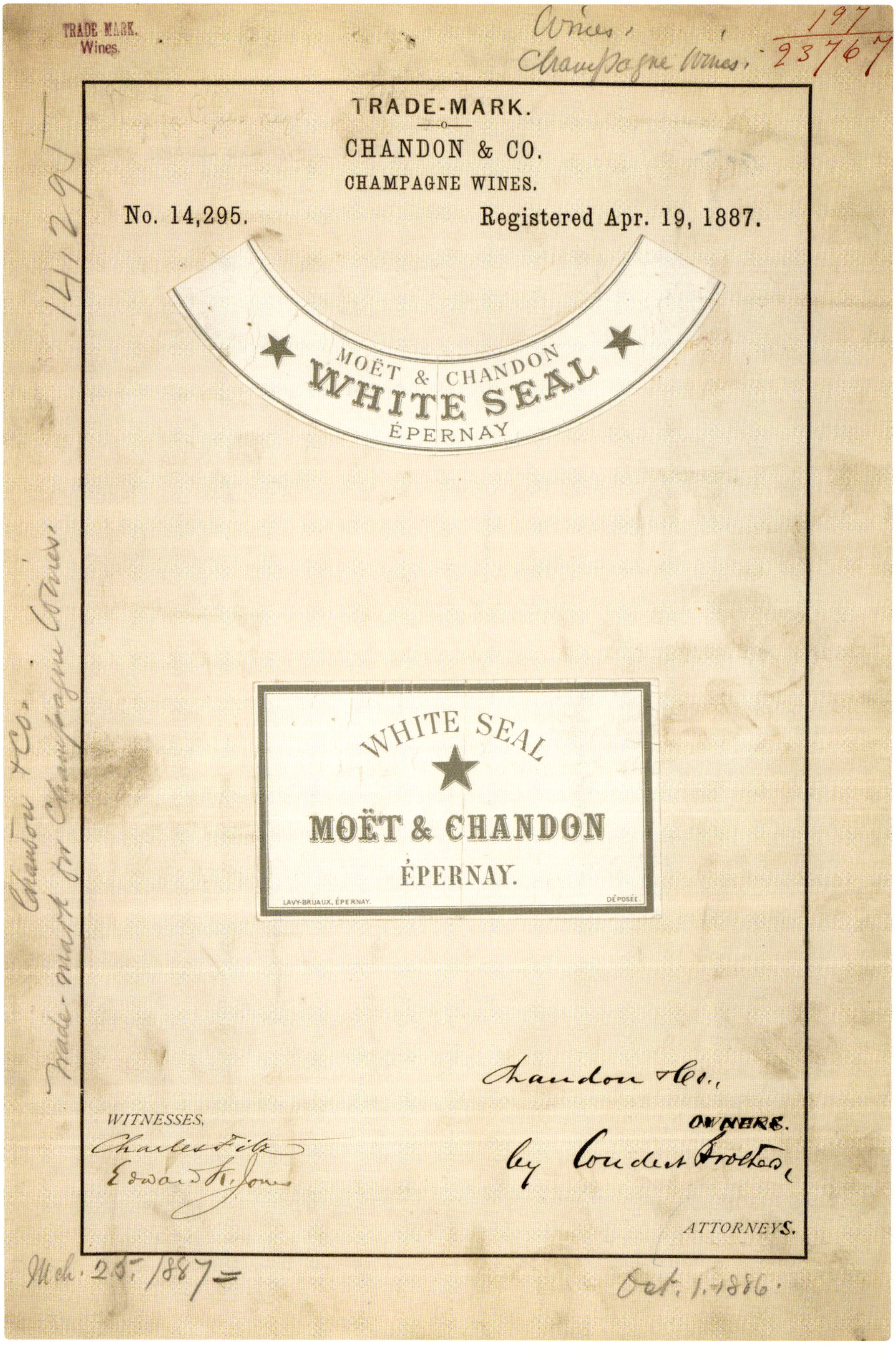

TRADE-MARK.
Wines.

Wines.
Champagne Wines.

197
23767

TRADE-MARK.

CHANDON & CO.

CHAMPAGNE WINES.

No. 14,295. Registered Apr. 19, 1887.

MOËT & CHANDON
WHITE SEAL
ÉPERNAY

WHITE SEAL
MOËT & CHANDON
ÉPERNAY.
LAVY-BRUAUX, ÉPERNAY. DÉPOSÉE.

14129

Chandon & Co.
Trade-mark for Champagne Wines.

Chandon & Co.,

WITNESSES,
Charles Fitz
Edward K. Jones

OWNERS.
by Coudert Brothers,

ATTORNEYS.

Mch. 25. 1887 =

Oct. 1. 1886.

Messieurs!! voulez_vous conquérir les cœurs!
OFFREZ LE
CHAMPAGNE
DE LA
JARRETIÈRE
Champagne de la Jarretière
Exiger la superbe PAIRE de JARRETIÈRES avec chaque bouteille

REVOLUTION AND STRIFE

Champagne entered the twentieth century with global sales approaching 35 million bottles, and demand rising at home and abroad. It seemed the best of all possible worlds – yet all was not well behind the scenes.

The name of 'champagne' was being traduced on a global scale, and within Champagne unscrupulous producers were undercutting the growers, or *vignerons*, by buying cheap base wine from the South. Meanwhile a tiny, sap-sucking aphid called phylloxera was slowly munching its way northwards through the vineyards of France.

In 1842, Charles Dickens encountered American 'champagne' made from sweetened turnips. Closer to home, there were 'champagnes' from the Loire, Burgundy, Italy and Spain. The campaign to stamp out these imposters led to the Union des Maisons de Champagne (UMC), founded in 1882. One of its aims was to "prevent the 'Champagne' name from being misused across the world". The issue was whether it was really a process or a region. When Josep Raventós, the pioneer of Spanish cava, promoted his wine as Cordoníu Champagne, was he ripping off the French or using a commonly understood term? The longer Cordoníu

Opposite: If imitation be the sincerest form of flattery, the Champenois refused to be flattered as they embarked on decades of litigation to stamp out imposters including this Spanish lookalike.

Left: A government edict excluding the Aube from the magic appellation of champagne, sparked protests across the region in the spring of 1911. "If we're not part of Champagne," cried one furious *vigneron*, "What are we? Part of the moon?"

and others did so, the greater the risk that champagne would become as generic as London Dry gin or Cheddar cheese.

Less contentious was the obvious opportunism of those producers who hired anyone with the right surname, from former cavalry officer Paul Ruinart to Strasbourg waiter Théophile Roederer. There was also Clicquot 'champagne' from Hungary, and a town in America that was rechristened Reims by a local producer. In Europe, the first framework for protecting a wine's geographic origin was established in 1890, though it took until 1905 to become law in France, paving the way for the *appellation contrôlée* system. When the issue came to the US courts, the UMC refused to pay for an American lawyer demanding US$15,000 if he lost and US$50,000 if he won. It's a decision that has haunted them ever since, given American stores still stock Californian champagne despite howls of protest from the French.

In 1890, phylloxera finally reached Champagne nearly 30 years after it was first spotted in southern France. It had devastated Bordeaux and other regions, yet the Champenois were ill prepared and complacent. At first the chalky soils seemed to offer protection and by 1898 only 50 hectares were affected. Within a decade, however, more than 30% of the Marne's vineyards had been wiped out. The solution – that of grafting the vines onto American rootstock – was already known, but it involved huge effort and expense. With global demand for champagne rising, merchants were forced further afield to source their base wine. Much was coming from the nearby Aube region halfway to Burgundy, while some was simply the cheapest plonk from the Midi.

Every autumn barrels of 'foreign' wine piled up at Épernay station while grape prices fell and the champagne chatelaines grew ever richer. In 1890 René Lamarre, the original champagne socialist, urged his 18,000 fellow *vignerons* to form a giant cooperative and share the riches, leaving the merchants with nothing. "Phylloxera isn't the only parasite in our vineyards," declared his pamphlet *La Révolution Champenoise*. He accused the merchants of being interested only in their brands, and predicted: "Within ten years we will no longer recognize the name of champagne."

Producers in the Aube were desperate to join Champagne, since Burgundy didn't want them and their trade with Paris had been lost to cheaper wines from the Midi. In 1908 official sales of champagne were almost 33 million bottles, while the Marne produced enough for just 16 million. That year the government set the boundaries of Champagne for the first time, excluding the Aube. "They've slit our throats," cried one local in despair. "If we're not part of Champagne, what are we? Part of the moon?"

Unfortunately most of the Aube was planted with local grapes of the Beaujolais variety, Gamay, which doesn't make good sparkling wine. A second government edict in February 1911 kept them out of Champagne, provoking mass demonstrations in the region. Local *vignerons* marched through the streets, armed with the hoes, or *fousseux*, they used to weed their vineyards. "Be strong and united," urged their leader Gaston Cheq, "there will be a gold mine ahead for you."

Two months later the government panicked and annulled the 1908 law, allowing the Aube to join Champagne and provoking an immediate, violent backlash in the Marne. It was the final straw after the worst harvest on record with truly pitiful yields. "One *vigneron* managed to make only a single bottle of wine, and that to keep as a souvenir," wrote Don and Petie Kladstrup in *Champagne – How the World's Most Glamorous Wine Triumphed Over War and Hard Times*. "Another picked so few grapes that all she could do was make a tart."

On the night of 11 April 1911, within hours of the government's decision, the Marne vineyards echoed to the sound of drums and bugles. The mob wreaked terror from one village to the next, burning cars, overturning trucks, breaking into cellars and smashing casks. Some 35,000 troops were drafted in overnight to quell the riot, but when the growers were blocked from entering Épernay, they attacked the nearby village of Aÿ. Buildings and vineyards were set on fire, while the streets flowed with wine. By 13 April it was all over, and amazingly no one had been killed.

WORLD WAR BLUES

The conflict that led to the champagne riots soon became nothing more than 'a little local difficulty' when compared to what developed during the summer of 1914. Within months the region found itself caught in the crossfire of the war to end all wars.

To maintain the peace after the Champagne riots, tens of thousands of troops were drafted into the region, and remained there until the harvest. After a spate of dismal vintages, 1911 saw a bumper harvest, and the authorities took advantage of the optimistic mood to declare the Aube could also produce champagne. It was to be called *Champagne deuxième zone*, or second division. Everyone knew it was a temporary fix, and the government was debating the issue yet again, when the assassination of Archduke Franz Ferdinand in Sarajevo in June 1914 changed everything.

Germany declared war on 3 August, and swept through the Low Countries into France in accordance with the Schlieffen Plan for a quick, decisive victory. Within weeks the people of Reims could hear the enemy's big guns approaching, and on 4 September the city was captured, followed by Épernay a day later. Part of the German army had crossed the River Marne and was within striking distance of Paris. The French government had fled to Bordeaux, leaving General Joseph Gallieni to defend the capital. Around midnight on 6 September he ordered Parisian taxi drivers to assemble in front of Les Invalides and ferry some 6,000 French troops to the front.

The convoy made its way east with headlights blacked out and meters running in time-honoured taxi tradition. The Battle of the Marne lasted a week and left an estimated half a million soldiers dead or wounded. The Germans retreated after their week-long occupation of Reims, to face the Allied forces across no man's land. The war that was supposed to be over by Christmas was now bogged down in the trenches that ran from the North Sea to Switzerland. The frontline cut through Champagne, and German guns in the hills beyond Reims continued to pound the city for the rest of the war.

The famous Reims Cathedral where so many French kings had been crowned was spared at first, but soon shells rained down reducing it to a burnt-out shell. This image became an important piece of anti-German propaganda, symbolising the barbarity of the Bosch. Many fled the city, while those who stayed disappeared into the *crayères*, the labyrinthine network of champagne tunnels. They were far more than just a refuge

from German bombs like the London Underground would be during the Blitz of the 1940s, and became a surreal subterranean universe that reflected life above ground before the war. There were shops, hospitals, church services, school lessons and even a few cows to provide milk. The tunnels "were bomb-proof and, when warmed with electricity or fuel stoves, proved by no means uncomfortable to live in," wrote Patrick Forbes in *Champagne: The Wine, the Land and the People*. "In fact many people," he concluded, "were so content underground that they did not come up for months at a time, and in certain cases for as long as two years." Reims was eventually evacuated, but when people returned there were just 40 houses still standing.

Despite the shelling and lack of manpower, grapes were picked every harvest throughout the war to produce a small, heroic vintage. Champagne Houses were badly shelled, including Ruinart, Lanson and Pommery. Meanwhile Mumm was seized by the French state because its owner, Hermann von Mumm, was interned in Brittany, having failed to take out French citizenship in time. As for the vineyards, 40% had been put out of action by shelling, gas and that seemingly indestructible aphid, phylloxera.

In 1919 a new French law reaffirmed the boundary of Champagne and decreed that only grapes grown in the region could be used. Reims was quickly rebuilt and the domestic trade picked up, at least in Paris with the Jazz Age in full swing. Legitimate trade with the States was snuffed out by Prohibition in 1920, though the 13 'dry' years saw at least 71 million bottles of champagne consumed according to a 'best guess estimate' by Don and Petie Kladstrup. Their book gives a vivid account of Jean-Charles Heidsieck's adventures supplying the underworld with fizz. The biggest risks were for the middlemen or rum-runners, while a bonus for suppliers like Heidsieck was the fact you didn't pay a cent of sales tax.

A year after Prohibition ended in 1933, Champagne enjoyed one of its best vintages for decades. Unfortunately the West was in the grip of the Great Depression and trade, both domestic and export, had collapsed. Grape prices fell from over 10 francs per kilo in 1926 to just 50 centimes and were barely worth picking. Producers decided to invoke the spirit of Dom Pérignon, by then a somewhat forgotten figure, and announced the 250th anniversary of the monk's 'invention' of champagne. Of more lasting impact was Dom Pérignon the brand, the first out and out luxury vintage champagne, released by Moët & Chandon in 1935.

Four years later the world was back at war, only this time the Champenois had eight months to hide thousands of bottles before the German invasion began in May 1940. The Nazis appointed Otto Klaebisch as *weinführer*, to extract as much champagne and profit as possible, while representing the industry was Count Robert-Jean de Vogüé, head of Moët & Chandon. He was also chief of the political wing of the French Resistance in eastern France and narrowly escaped the death penalty in 1943. There were countless tales of heroism, and the tunnels of many Champagne Houses were used to hide Resistance fighters and stash arms dropped by the Allies. But as a region, the damage was nothing compared to the previous conflict. According to Nicholas Faith in *The Story of Champagne*, there were just a couple of air raids and a few bombs accidentally dropped on Aÿ by an American airman, during the entire war.

Opposite (left): Bombed damage to the Place Royale in Reims during War World One.

Opposite (right): Comte Robert-Jean de Vogüé, Moët & Chandon's inspirational boss and industry leader during the German occupation in World War II. He escaped the death sentence and survived years in the notorious Ziegenhain labour camp.

Above: "I confirm I have arrived safely" ran the caption on this cartoon postcard of two GIs soaking up the nightlife in Paris after the city's liberation in August 1944.

Overleaf: The bomb-damaged Cathedral of Notre-Dame de Reims, which was then painstakingly restored and reopened in 1938.

THE ASCENDANCE OF CHAMPAGNE

The first half of the twentieth century was difficult not only for champagne but the world in general. Such was the impact of two world wars, the Great Depression and US prohibition that champagne sales recovered to their 1913 level of 35 million bottles only in the mid-1950s.

During this period the industry consolidated and some once famous names disappeared, while many of the growers had joined cooperatives owned by their members. At first the co-ops produced only base wine, or *vin clair*, but under pressure to do more, they merged into larger unions of cooperatives where they had the scale to invest in cellars and bottling lines. In time they began supplying the supermarkets with own-brand champagne, or selling it on the open market in a practice known as *sur latte*.

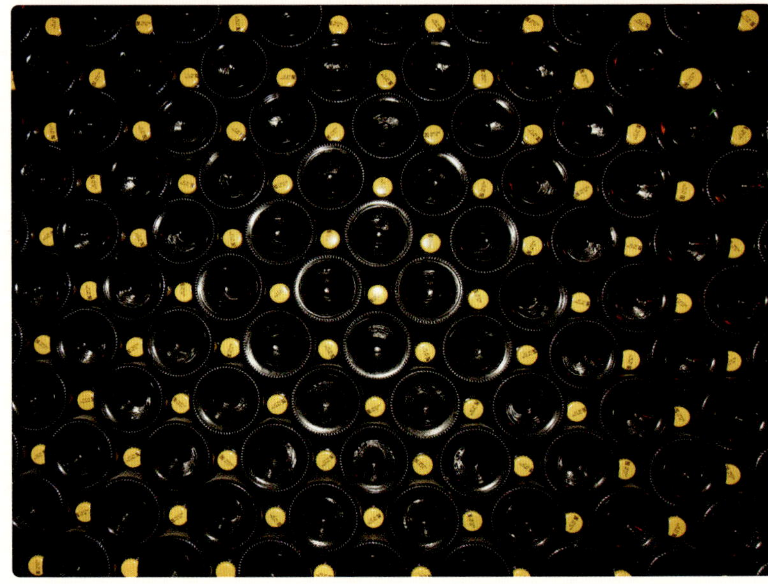

The latte are the thin wooden strips between the rows of bottles ageing in the cellar, and wines sold *sur latte* are in unlabelled bottles yet to be disgorged. They are bought by merchants who will slap on a label as though they were the producer, having done nothing more than disgorge the wines and decide on the level of *dosage*. Like those tartan rugs from Pakistan labelled 'hand-finished in Scotland', there's a distinct whiff of deception about *sur latte* with the consumer left blissfully unaware. It is the real commodity end of the champagne trade, and despite repeated calls for a ban, it continues to this day.

Out of the war came the Comité Interprofessionel du vin de Champagne, or CIVC, founded in 1941. Before each harvest it would set grape prices according to the strength of the market and whether or not the vineyards were rated Grands Crus, Premier Crus or Deuxième Crus. Since 1990 this rigid system was replaced with a free-trade negotiation between the Champagne Houses and the growers. The CIVC is also charged with providing technical support, enforcing the rules, promoting the wines and the region, and protecting the champagne 'brand'. The first big victory in the courts was over Spanish 'champagne' in the 1950s. Since then, with the exception of a few 'champagne' brands in the US, the CIVC's lawyers have gradually squeezed out other imposters while clamping down on 'parasite products' from 'champagne' soaps to Babycham. Perhaps their greatest coup was having the expression *méthode champenoise* banned in the EU in 1992. At a stroke there was clear blue water between champagne and that woefully generic term – sparkling wine.

The first big post-war market to emerge took everyone by surprise. Domestic consumption had grown five-fold by the late 1970s and accounted for two-thirds of all champagne, in complete contrast to the

start of the century. Almost half the wine was coming from the grower producers, or *récoltant manipulants*, whom the French, and especially the Parisians, loved to buy from. For these small producers it meant cash in hand and no need to go through a costly distribution chain, while for the consumer it was a chance to deal direct with the family who made the champagne, or so it seemed. In reality the wine was often the non-vintage Brut from the local co-op to which the grower belonged. He had simply labelled some stock that he had bought, that possibly contained one or two of his grapes.

Within the vineyards, the outlying areas of Aisne and the Aube had been transformed. In the 1950s more than four-fifths of the Aube was planted with the Beaujolais grape Gamay, which had been used to make poor-quality fizz and that seemed to confirm the region's second-class status. Over a number of decades these were ripped out and replaced with the three champagne grapes, causing the Aube to lose the stigma of being considered the Marne's poor relation.

The surge in domestic champagne sales helped change the structure of the trade. The cooperatives expanded rapidly during the 1960s and by 1990 accounted for over half of all the growers and a third of all the vineyards in Champagne. As the co-ops merged into powerful cooperative unions, the number of family-owned merchants also began to contract. In 1963 Moët & Chandon began to acquire rivals, starting with Ruinart, the oldest House of all, followed by Mercier in 1970. Moët then merged with Hennessy, the leading Cognac House, and afterwards with the fashion company Louis Vuitton to form LVMH, which added Krug to the portfolio in 1999. The same corporate fate befell Mumm, Heidsieck Monopole, Lanson and Pommery, leaving only a handful of the old guard in family hands.

Export markets began to catch up with the surge in French sales, though progress was slow at first. Recalling his first sales trip to America in the 1960s, Pol Roger's Christian de Billy found people "had lost the habit of drinking champagne", as retold by Don Hewitson in *The Glory of Champagne*. Twenty years later, America became the biggest importer of champagne, a title it soon lost to the UK. But, as of 2023, almost 27 million bottles were shipped to the US, followed by the UK on 25.5 million, and Japan on 15.3 million.

A generation ago, these were undreamt-of numbers for champagne. The big players had become supremely confident in their brands to the extent of setting up satellite operations like Domaine Chandon and Mumm Cuvée Napa. Yet there were always periodic crises, notably the recession of the early 1990s when sales fell and Champagne was awash with unsold stock. According to the champagne expert, Tom Stevenson, one economist even suggested the growers leave the grapes unpicked for a harvest to drain the surplus. Luckily the advice was ignored, for the world was gearing up to the biggest New Year's Eve party ever.

Opposite (top): In the smaller Champagne Houses automation was slow to arrive and staff at Pommery's cellars, near Reims, were still wrapping the bottles of champagne by hand in 1956.

Opposite (bottom): Bottles lying *sur latte* (on slats) in the Taittinger cellars. The corks apart, there are no labels attached to the bottles so the seller will, after the disgorgement, put them on the market as if they were the maker.

Above: Three of the best-known champagne brands, Veuve Clicquot, Moët & Chandon and Krug, are now all part of the the world's largest luxury goods maker, LVMH, Luis Vuitton Moët Hennessy.

THE NEW MILLENNIUM

For once, an era dawned full of hope and expectation. The only blip on the radar was a predicted event that fortunately never happened, and this allowed the biggest global party ever to take place without a hitch.

As the clock ticked towards midnight, 31 December 1999, there were dire warnings of a computer meltdown with planes falling from the sky. Almost worse was the prospect of no champagne. The region had been pumping up production to 270 million bottles a year since the mid-1990s and the CIVC had sanctioned the release of 132 million bottles of reserve wine. Yet still the gloomy prediction of a champagne drought days, hours, before D-day hung in the air. But, in the end, all was well, the internet didn't crash and the famous fizz flowed through the night.

With the morning after came the hangover, at least for those in the wine trade taken in by all the speculation and hype. In the year before, UK imports of champagne were up by one-third, while sales rose by only 19%. The supermarket Sainsbury's was said to be drowning in 800,000 surplus bottles of its own-label Blanc de Noirs. Over the Easter weekend it slashed the price to £5.99 and made a loss of £4 on every bottle, or so it was rumoured. Back in Champagne, however, it was simply a chance to replenish stocks and ride out the inevitable post-Millennial dip.

Within two or three years, sales were back at record levels and growing at over 5% annually. Despite a series of bountiful vintages as in 2004, the supply of grapes was being stretched to the limit. "Yields are at a maximum, and we will soon have our backs to the wall," cried Moët & Chandon's then CEO, Fréderic Cumenal, in 2007. His prayers were answered that August with reports of trouble in the US subprime mortgage market. The consequences took a while to sink in, and initially there were doubts that it would spread to the so-called 'real economy'.

But spread it did, as credit lines froze and greed turned to fear in the financial markets. Global champagne sales tumbled from a 2007 all-time high of 338 million bottles to around 300 million. The age of conspicuous consumption was officially over, or at least on hold, and even the wealthiest bankers were now sipping it discreetly. But writing in his

2009 book *The Finest Wines of Champagne*, Michael Edwards wondered if: "The cold douche of market forces ... may yet turn out to be a blessing in disguise for Champagne, dampening sales expectations and bringing a new mood of sober reflection to a bull market that risks losing control of prices."

Back in 2003, it was decided to look at expanding Champagne – not by extending the outer perimeter but by granting a number of villages within it the right to produce the wine. Given the impact on land prices and the dynamics of supply and demand, it was a highly sensitive issue and was sensibly left to experts at the INAO, who govern the country's wine appellations. Eventually, 45 villages were chosen to join the existing 319, while two were to be evicted.

There were howls of protest from these two and all the other villages that had hoped to join the club and subsequently see their land prices soar to perhaps €1.5 million a hectare (as of 2019), compared to no more than €30,000 outside Champagne. That year, *The Times* quoted an unnamed mayor saying, "Imagine that one farmer gets the right to make champagne and his neighbour does not. How do you think they are going to settle that? They're going to get out the guns." So far no one's been shot, and the INAO is still working on the 280,000 plots attached to the lucky villages. A final decision, after another tsunami of appeals, is not expected until 2030.

Meanwhile, in the decade after the 2008 financial crash, sales recovered until the Covid pandemic of 2020–21 threatened disaster. "One could hardly pick a tougher test for Champagne than an invisible threat that prompts a societal shutdown," wrote Patrick Schmitt MW in the *Drinks Business*. "After all, sparkling wine is the default up-market option for good times – and it's consumed socially."

But demand proved remarkably resilient, down by just a fifth in 2020 – perhaps champagne "has become a tipple to turn to as life becomes sour, not just when everything's sweet," wondered Schmitt. Sales then exploded in a great post-pandemic party that lasted two years until the euphoria fizzled out, and for now the region believes it has found a sweet spot of selling around 300 million bottles a year for a turnover of €6 billion or more.

To help manage supply – and smooth out the wild swings in the size of the vintage – the Champagne authorities have devized an ingenious system of reserves. Each summer the winegrowers and the Champagne Houses set the 'yield' for the coming harvest based on current and forecast demand, among other factors. If Mother Nature is bountiful, the excess has to be stored separately and can only be released when the authorities say so. If the harvest comes in short, producers may be allowed to draw on this, as well as their own personal reserves. The system also seeks to keep stock levels balanced, ideally to around three years' worth in the region's cellars.

Not all champagne is as good as it should be, but overall standards have risen, and this is perhaps most noticeable in the vineyards themselves. The race to keep up with demand has seen plantings treble since the 1950s, yet production has increased ten-fold. Powerful fertilizers and pesticides combined with more vigorous rootstocks and vines, ramped

up average yields. Visitors used to report seeing vineyards sprayed by men in what looked like fall-out suits. Go back further, and there were *bleus de ville*, or blue bags, full of Parisian rubbish strewn over the ground as compost – so much for champagne's glamorous image.

But the bin bags have long gone, and the use of chemical fertilizers, pesticides and fungicides has been cut in half since 2001. Today, "almost all the vineyards are protected by sexual confusion," says Brigitte Batonnet, the CIVC's press officer, about pheromone capsules that befuddle the poor male butterfly as he tries to mate. Since the 2003 heat wave, which led to the first-ever harvest in August, talk of climate change has grown louder. Yet rather than rising temperatures, it is the rise in pests and diseases that concerns many. *Flavescence dorée*, a new bacterial disease spread by leafhoppers and first spotted in France in Armagnac in 1949, has now reached Champagne. Chardonnay is particularly susceptible, and, with no cure as yet, it has been dubbed 'the phylloxera of the new century'.

Organic vineyards, while growing, still account for less than 10% of the total in this generally cool, damp region on the edge of plant wine. Much more popular has been the VDC certification (*Viticulture Durable en Champagne*), which now accounts for 45% of vineyards. The CIVC has decreed that all vineyards must be certified in some way by 2030 in its bid to make Champagne one of the greenest wine regions in France.

Opposite: Grapes growing on the hilly vineyards of Philipponnat, in Mareuil-sur-Ay. They are considered to be one of the greenest of all the Champagne Houses.

Above: Lanson has exclusively provided the champagne to serve up with the strawberries and cream at the Wimbledon Championships.

CHAMPAGNE
MERCIER
EPERNAY
POMMER
REIMS
VERTUS
HENRI
FRANCE
REIMS

3

ON THE CHAMPAGNE ROUTE

It is time to leave the history of the region and explore champagne through the great Houses that made it a byword for luxury around the world. Behind the brands and those of the big cooperatives are the thousands of growers, and beyond them the sea of sparkling wine made in champagne's image.

BILLECART-SALMON
MAREUIL-SUR-AŸ

Famed for its sublime, delicate rosés, Billecart-Salmon is still family-owned and family-run and now in its seventh generation under Mathieu Roland-Billecart. "Our strategic focus is quality, and doing things right," he says. "Quality is what you do when people are not watching."

The animal gracing the Billecart family's seventeenth-century coat of arms is not a leaping salmon, but a greyhound at full stretch beneath three bunches of grapes. The arms were authorised to Pierre Billecart by Louis XIII, and it was his descendant, Nicolas François, who founded Champagne Billecart in 1818.

The House has always been based in the pretty village of Mareuil-sur-Aÿ where Nicolas François, a local lawyer, had vineyards. To these were added six hectares of vines in the Côte des Blancs, belonging to Elisabeth Salmon's family when she married him in the 1820s. A generation or two later the families split and the old Salmon vineyards were sold off at auction in Épernay. The Billecarts tried to drop the 'S' word from the label, but the trade informed them that it was too late – their champagne was too well-known as Billecart-Salmon, and so the name stuck.

Charles Heidsieck, aka Champagne Charlie, has always taken the credit for pioneering the US market for champagne but he first crossed the Atlantic in 1852, 20 years after Billecart opened its first overseas office in New York. This nugget of family history comes from sixth-generation Antoine Rolland-Billecart, deputy general manager in charge of exports. Quite what happened to the New York office is a mystery.

Antoine believes that Billecart, like other Houses, began by producing still wine. "It was village wine like in Burgundy, and was both red and white," he says. "The bubbles came a bit later." By the 1870s Billecart-

Salmon was undoubtedly sparkling and was exclusive supplier to the court of King Ludwig II of Bavaria, yet there is still a focus on what lies beneath the fizz. "We always want to remind you that champagne is a wine," says Antoine.

Billecart-Salmon was almost snuffed out by the Second World War. Mareuil-sur-Aÿ found itself caught in the conflict in 1944 between advancing American troops and Germans attempting to dig in. Antoine's father Jean had been deported to a labour camp in Germany for two and a half years, and when released it took him six weeks to get back from Berlin to the village. The impulse to quit the business was strong, but in 1947 he and his father began to rebuild the House slowly, focusing on the domestic market at the start. Production gradually increased from around 300,000 bottles to over 2 million today. Exports spread slowly outwards to Belgium and Italy and reached the UK thanks to a pioneering importer: Mark Savage of Windrush Wines.

In 1954, Billecart-Salmon was one of the first producers to believe in rosé, which at Billecart is always referred to as 'champagne rosé' and not the other way round. The idea is that if blindfolded you wouldn't be able to tell its colour from the taste. Knowing how good the still red wine could be from villages like Bouzy and Mareuil, the method was always to blend it in with the white juice rather than let colour bleed in from the skins in the classic way of making a still rosé. That method may be perfect for a crisp salty Provençal rosé, but it risks adding tannin to the wine, which Billecart studiously avoid.

Either way it has become one of the most admired rosés in Champagne, though back in 1954 Billecart's neighbours thought they had lost the plot. At the time, rosé accounted for less than 4% of total production and was dismissed by many. Some of the grandees of champagne swore they would never make a pink wine. Today, of course, they all do.

Meanwhile the family created a beautiful garden with flowers and fruit trees at their home in Mareuil and in 1964 began planting pinot noir in the parkland beyond to produce a few precious bottles of Clos Saint-Hilaire Blanc de Noirs. The first vintage was in 1995, and today this pure-bred pinot, which would have once been a still wine used for rosé, is completely biodynamic, with a yield typically around half the average in Champagne.

A third of Billecart-Salmon's 100 hectare estate is owned by the family, with the remainder of grapes purchased from vineyards where they maintain control of viticulture. Half the vines are in Grand Cru vineyards.

Opposite: Billecart's cellar, where its Sous Bois (under oak) wines are fermented in the traditional style in large wooden vats. Sous Bois was first released in 2011.

Above (left): The founder of the dynasty – Nicolas François Billecart – the lawyer who established Champagne Billecart in 1818.

Above (right): Nicolas' wife, Elisabeth Salmon, who contributed six hectares of vineyards to the family business. Her side of the family later split and moved back to Normandy, but the name lived on.

TASTING NOTES

LE RÉSERVE

Billecart's flagship may be its delicate salmon-pink rosé, but its Brut Reserve, a blend of pinot noir, chardonnay and pinot meunier, is equally alluring. There are clean, fresh notes of pears and subtle, pastry-like aromas. With over three years of ageing on the lees, there's a nutty, toasty edge to the fruit on the tongue. In future the ageing will extend to 50 months.

BILLECART-SALMON CUVÉE NICOLAS FRANÇOIS BILLECART 2002

First created in 1964, as a tribute to the House's founder, this prestige cuvée has a brilliant golden hue, a testament to its age and to being partially vinified in oak. The fruit, a blend of Grand Cru chardonnay and pinot noir, has the feintest hint of sweetness – that of candied peel and rose petals, and is said to be perfect with lemon sole cooked in butter.

BOLLINGER
AŸ

Fiercely independent and as 'British' as James Bond, Bollinger has been a remarkable story of survival. Established in 1829, it is one of those rare Champagne Houses still in family hands. The fact that its vineyards supply two-thirds of its needs must be one reason why.

Bollinger is truly part of the Establishment thanks to its readily pronounceable name and unbroken string of royal warrants from Queen Victoria to the present day. It courses through the veins of James Bond, and it flowed through the Oxford of Evelyn Waugh, who renamed the Bullingdon Club the 'Bollinger Club' in *Decline and Fall*. In the latter half of the twentieth century "Bring out the Bolly!" became a regular Friday-night call from City traders to Sloane Rangers.

It is tempting to imagine some nineteenth-century Lord Bollinger stopping off in France on return from his Grand Tour, and founding a Champagne House to supply his friends back home. The style clearly appealed to the Brits who were drinking 85% of sales before the Second World War. In truth, however, the roots of the firm are German – not unlike those of the British Royal Family.

Born in Württemberg, Joseph Bollinger was employed as a salesman by the aristocratic de Villermont family in Aÿ along with a local, Paul-Joseph Renaudin. The family had lived there since the fifteenth century and owned 11 hectares of vineyards in Aÿ and Cuis. They decided to launch a champagne of their own, but because they did not want their name on the bottles, maybe thinking it was vulgar, the House of Renaudin-Bollinger & Cie was founded in 1829.

Athanase de Villermont was the third partner, but he died three years later. Bollinger wasted no time expanding the existing vineyards, buying a third one in Verzenay and, crucially, marrying de Villermont's daughter, Louise-Charlotte, in 1837. Renaudin died without an heir in 1854, though his name remained on the label for more than a century. Joseph Bollinger and Louis-Charlotte were left in charge and their descendants still own the business. Keeping family shareholders in check and corporate predators at bay cannot have been easy. Yet owning 165 hectares of vineyards as it does today, 85% of them grand and premier cru, must have been a useful buffer in bad times.

Bollinger opened a London office in 1850, which was later absorbed into the wine importers Mentzendorff. Within 40 years Mentzendorff, now owned by Bollinger, was handling almost all the sales with 89% in the UK and 7% going to the British Empire. At Victorian and Edwardian shooting parties, it was known as 'the Boy' – a reference to the young lad who would follow the guns with a pony laden with Bollinger so they could slake their thirst amidst the slaughter. Today the UK accounts for just one-tenth of the sales.

In 1911, Bollinger released its Special Cuvée (SV) for the UK, and its fulsome, rich yet dry character came to epitomise the House style. Today SV is around 60% pinot noir, 15% pinot meunier and 25% chardonnay with half the wines barrel-fermented to give a slight oakiness to the finish. SV is aged on its lees for at least three years, with typically one-tenth added from reserve wines up to 15 years old.

When Jacques Bollinger died in the Second World War, his Scottish wife Lilly was left in charge. She was another strong matriarch in the Veuve Clicquot mould who helped restore the business, and launch the innovative Bollinger RD ('recently disgorged') in 1961. As a vintage expression it showed what a decade's ageing on the lees could achieve.

Her nephew, Christian Bizot, helped broker the deal with the Bond producer Cubby Broccoli, to get Bollinger in bed with 007 [see page 145] and build a very fruitful relationship. Later the British hit television comedy *Absolutely Fabulous* had dipsomaniac Patsy Stone (Joanna Lumley) living on a cocktail of 'Bolly' and 'Stoli'. "The last mosquito that bit me," she once slurred, "had to check into the Betty Ford clinic." Despite concerns that the brand was being trashed, it seems all publicity is good publicity.

Bollinger's MD Charles-Armand de Belenet senses a shift in Champagne from the branded approach of Bordeaux with its big châteaux to something "nearer to Burgundy with its focus on terroir and villages," he told the *Drinks Business*. And, thanks to climate change, he believes the region will also be able to produce "outstanding still wines in the coming years".

Opposite (left): Bollinger's imposing headquarters in Aÿ with its façade lit up at night. The House is a pillar of the champagne establishment and a quintessential Grande Marque.

Opposite (right): A trade card for 'Bollinger's Champagne' from the 1890s, proudly displaying its royal warrants of appointment to Queen Victoria and Edward, Prince of Wales.

Above: Crates of Bollinger Champagne being unloaded at Sheerness Docks in England in 1965. Before the Second World War, the British were drinking 85% of Bollinger's sales.

TASTING NOTES

LA GRANDE ANNÉE 2015

This blend of 11 crus is led by pinot noir from Verzenay, Aÿ and Mareuil-sur-Aÿ, supported by chardonnay from Chouilly and Avize, which makes up 40% of the wine. There is a whisp of vanilla amongst the crunchy red fruit on the nose, and a richness in the mid-palate before it sharpens on the finish.

PN VZ 19

This pure-bred pinot noir comes from some of Bollinger's more northerly vineyards around Verzenay. It is bright and golden on the eye, and its aromas are rich, complex and impossible to tease apart. It is fruity and generous in the mouth, drying to a long, slightly saline finish.

DOM PÉRIGNON
HAUTVILLERS

Whenever the 'Dom' is mentioned in hushed tones by well-heeled champagnistas, they are talking of the bottled version not the famous benedictine monk. Born in the 1930s, Dom Pérignon was long the pinnacle of Moët & Chandon, but in recent decades has developed its own separate identity.

"Hautvillers Abbey – birthplace of champagne" declares Dom Pérignon's website in bold capitals. It continues:

"This is the place where Dom Pierre Pérignon dedicated 47 years of his life to invent and perfect the techniques to create a wine whose reputation knows no equal."

Note the word 'techniques', for he certainly did not invent champagne as we know it.

Dom Pierre Pérignon pushed the art of winemaking to a level it had never reached before in Champagne. While cellarmaster at Hautvillers, he implemented precise viticulture techniques to improve the grapes' quality. He leveraged the art of blending with grapes coming from different crus, and he introduced the gentle and fractional pressing to obtain white wines from black grapes. What he did not do was invent the world's most famous sparkling wine.

The myth of Dom Pérignon, who died in 1715, was created much later. It was given a lift when Pierre-Gabriel Chandon, who had just married Adelaïde Moët, acquired the vineyards and defunct abbey of Hautvillers in the 1820s. But the big boost came in 1932. With champagne sales in the doldrums during the Depression, the Champenois decided to celebrate the 250th anniversary of the Dom's great 'invention'. It was a pretty arbitrary date, but it achieved its aim of stimulating demand.

That same year, at a meeting of the Syndicat of Champagne Houses, a PR man called Lawrence Venn suggested someone should launch a real luxury brand. Given the state of the global economy it sounded as daft as Marie Antoinette's famous declaration: "Let them eat cake", and the idea was quickly shot down. But it caught the attention of Robert-Jean de Voguë, who was there as Moët & Chandon's newly appointed sales director. He took Venn out to dinner and hatched a plan to create Dom Pérignon.

The champagne Dom Pérignon was launched in London in 1935, using a replica of an eighteenth-century bottle with an imposing shield for a

label. It was a Cuvée Centenaire marking not Dom Pérignon's birthday, but the 100th anniversary of Moët & Chandon's first agency abroad, Simon Brothers. They wanted a special wine as a gift for their 100 top customers.

It was from the 1926 vintage and interestingly didn't carry the famous name. Word of its existence reached America and the following year a shipment of just 100 cases was despatched to New York aboard the luxury French liner, the *Normandie*. This time it was from the older, highly rated 1921 vintage, and did carry the name Dom Pérignon. The rest, as they say, is history.

Louis Roederer with Cristal might dispute that 'the Dom' was the first ever prestige cuvée, but it is the wine that other Houses have sought to copy. Unlike Krug's Grande Cuvée or Taittinger's Comtes de Champagne, however, it has always been a vintage wine. How much is produced today is a closely guarded secret, and estimates vary wildly from 3.5–8 million bottles. It is almost entirely sourced from Moët's own vineyards with a roughly equal blend of chardonnay from Grand Cru villages like Avize and Cramant, and pinot noir from the best sites in Aÿ, Ambonay, Bouzy and the like. In all some 21 villages contribute.

In 1971, it was joined by a rosé whose first vintage was 1959. Among the first to enjoy it were world leaders who joined the Shah of Iran to celebrate the 2,500th anniversary of the Persian Empire. The party in Persepolis reputedly cost over US$100 million. Today Dom Pérignon Rosé accounts for a fraction of total sales, and usually costs at least double the main expression.

Initially Dom Pérignon was released in roughly two out of every five vintages, but since 1997 only the 2001 was not released. Richard Geoffroy, Dom Pérignon's previous, long-standing *chef de cave*, committed to producing the wine annually, albeit in much reduced quantities in difficult years. Interpreting the unique character of the seasons involves elements of risk, particularly with an increasingly erratic climate.

For Vincent Chaperon, who succeeded as *chef de cave* in 2019, the key to overcoming these challenges lies in having access to 900 hectares of premier and Grand Cru vineyards to make the best selection each year. Chaperon is obsessive about picking the precise harvest date for each plot, and when it comes to tasting the still wines to make the assemblage, he believes texture and mouthfeel are the most important factors.

Opposite (top): The Abbey Saint-Pierre, in Hautvillers. Dom Pierre Pérignon was appointed cellar master in 1668.

Opposite (below): A much photographed statue of Dom Pérignon, clutching a foaming bottle of his great 'invention', outside the headquarters of Moët & Chandon in Épernay.

Above: Estimates of the wine's annual production vary wildly from 3.5 million to 8 million bottles, but the true figure remains a closely guarded secret.

Overleaf: Panoramic shot of the Dom Perignon vinyards, the town of Hautvillers and the surrounding lands.

TASTING NOTES

DOM PÉRIGNON 2015

The year of 2015 was a hot, dry one in Champagne, but this wine that was finally disgorged eight years later is full of silky-textured, ripe fruit coupled with DP's tell-tale flinty note. It has a creamy mousse, but a sharp, citrus edge to keep it clean and well-defined. This almost equal blend of pinot noir and chardonnay has a dosage of just 4.5 gms/litre.

DOM PÉRIGNON P2 1998

P2 signifies a second release of this vintage with even longer on the lees and a slightly lower dosage. The result will delight lovers of that bready, yeasty character of old champagne, with all the brioche and shortbread aromas you could wish for. There's marzipan and hazelnuts, yet a vibrant, lemony freshness too.

GOSSET
AŸ

Gosset has been making wine in the village of Aÿ since the sixteenth century. Until the advent of strong bottles made of English glass one assumes it was all still wine. Yet, more than 440 years later, this fine boutique maison is still going strong under its new ownership.

Dom Pérignon was not even a twinkle in his grandmother's eye when Pierre Gosset set up his wine business in Aÿ in 1584. The village was just down the road from the Dom's abbey and at the time much more famous for its wines than Hautvillers. Consider that Francis I of France and Henry VIII of England both kept cellars in the village. Indeed, Francis decreed he was not just king of France, but also *Roi d'Aÿ et de Gonesse* (King of Aÿ and Gonesse – the latter being a town famed for its flour).

So why then let Ruinart bask in the glory of being 'the first Champagne House', founded 145 years later in 1729? Well, it all comes down to a question of definition. Gosset claims only to be the first 'Wine House', and until some evidence is unearthed of an early departure into bottles that sparkled, one has to assume its production was entirely of still wine. Not that Ruinart can prove it was producing fizz from day one, but according to the current MD, Jean-Pierre Cointreau: "there's a very precise agreement between the two Houses". It is clearly one they both respect.

As with just about every Champagne House before the early nineteenth century, no one bothered to document the moment of transition from still to sparkling champagne, or if they did the records have long disappeared. What is remarkable about the Gosset family, given the Napoleonic Code of subdividing inheritance between siblings, is that the last Gosset was still running the business as late as 1994.

This was Etienne Gosset, whose father had used his fortune from the sale of the Rochas perfume company, where he was a key partner, to buy control of the House. However, given there had been sixteen generations since Pierre Gosset, the vineyard holdings had been scattered between a veritable army of cousins. By the mid-1980s the House owned just 10 hectares, having made a killing selling off some prime sites to Krug the previous decade, while production was a modest 250,000 bottles.

When Gosset was sold to its present owners – Groupe Renauld Cointreau – in 1994, it came with just a hectare of vines. "Of course financially speaking you are better off owning vineyards," says Jean-

Below (left): Gosset's offices in Aÿ, where François I of France and Henry VIII of England kept wine cellars. Both kings died in 1547, and 37 years later Pierre Gosset started his family wine business in the village.

Below (right): The House currently produces around 1.1 million bottles a year, 40% of which is its highly rated Grande Reserve.

Pierre Cointreau. "However, champagne is a blend of different wines from different areas, and we work with 160 growers, some who have been supplying Gosset for three generations. So the advantage of not having vineyards is that it gives you this diversity and you can really create the blend as you wish."

The Cointreau family own Frapin Cognac, and though they came as outsiders to Champagne, there was one vital thread of continuity from the days of Etienne Gosset. That thread was the late *chef de cave*, Jean-Pierre Mareigner, a true local from Aÿ, who spent almost his entire career at Gosset, having joined in 1983, aged 27. His father had been vineyard director beforehand. That role has been taken up by Odilon de Varine, who joined as deputy-MD in 2006, having been cellarmaster at Deutz and Henriot beforehand. "At Gosset we first create a wine. The bubbles make it sublime," he says, adding that its champagnes "are famous for being full-bodied yet very elegant by avoiding malo-lactic fermentation so that the wines keep all their natural fruitiness and freshness".

Gosset is still very much a boutique Champagne House, though annual production has increased to around 1.1 million bottles. Since 2009, there has been plenty of scope for future growth since buying from Laurent-Perrier an impressive winery and 1.7 kms of cellars in Épernay next door to Pol Roger. These, and its surrounding parkland, are open to visitors.

The move to Épernay has given Gosset the luxury of space, where it can give its top wines, including Compte-d'Age and Gosset Celebris, as much ageing on the lees as it wishes. Some 40% of its production is its highly rated Grande Reserve that, like all Gosset wines, is bottled in a bulbous, slender-necked copy of an eighteenth-century bottle.

Left: The bulbous thin-necked bottles used for champagne in the eighteenth century have been faithfully copied for Gosset.

TASTING NOTES

GOSSET GRANDE RÉSERVEBRUT NV

While there is a more entry-level 'Brut Excellence', it's really worth stretching to the much-admired Grande Réserve. All Champagne Houses boast of elegance and finesse, but this wine has it in spades along with a whiff of spice and the faintest trace of digestive biscuits through bottle age.

GOSSET CELEBRIS 2012

Gosset only release this vintage expression every four years on average. The 2012 is 70% chardonnay from some of the best villages of the Côte des Blancs, and after ten years of bottle ageing it has a delightful structure and depth of fruit, while the texture and mousse are just perfect.

HENRIOT
REIMS

Henriot's founder, Apolline Godinot, was a classic champagne widow in the mold of her early nineteenth-century contemporary, Barbe Nicole Clicquot Ponsardin. If Henriot is not quite as famous as Veuve Clicquot, though its reputation has been rising steadily in recent decades.

In 1794 Apolline married Nicolas Henriot, from a long line of drapers in Reims, and brought with her some Pinot Noir vineyards in the Montagne de Reims. With this dowry and on her husband's death in 1808, she founded Maison Henriot. In 1851 Appoline's grandson Ernest Henriot took time out to help his cousin Charles Heidsieck with his Champagne House. By the time he returned to Henriot in 1875 it was supplying the Dutch Court, and went on to supply the Hapsburg dynasty in its twilight years. The making of the estate was the marriage of Ernest's son Paul to Marie Marguet from the Côte des Blancs in 1880 which brought with it three cru vineyards of chardonnay.

The bond with Heidsieck was finally cemented a century later by Joseph Henriot who bought the House, only to sell it on to Rémy Martin in 1985. He was, by all accounts, a consummate deal-maker, and not just in Champagne. Having absorbed Heidsieck, Joseph proceeded to sell almost the entire Henriot estate to LVMH. The luxury goods giant gained 125 hectares, including a swathe of valuable vineyards in the Côte des Blancs in return for an 11% share in Veuve Clicquot. As the largest individual share-holder, he became the boss and is credited with building Veuve Clicquot into a global brand before leaving the company in 1994 to turn his attention to restoring the somewhat neglected House of Henriot.

As part of the deal with LVMH, Henriot lost all its Grand Cru holdings in the Côte des Blancs and now owns just 35 hectares in all. These include 12 in Chouilly – Grand Cru for chardonnay – and 11 in Aÿ, Mareuil- sur-Aÿ and Avenay. While Joseph Henriot focussed on expanding his wine empire into Burgundy, buying the négociant, Bouchard Père et Fils, followed by William Fevre in Chablis, his son Stanislas was left to run the champagne business in 1999. Joseph died in 2015, leaving Maisons & Domaine Henriot to be chaired by his nephew, Gilles de Larouzière.

Despite all the changes at the top, and the focus on building Henriot's export markets, the wines themselves have not been neglected thanks in large part to the talents of Laurent Fresnet who was Henriot's highly regarded cellar master for 13 years. The son of a local grower, with wine-making experience in the New World, he wanted to sharpen up the House style when he took on the role in 2006. "What we changed was to be much more mineral, more fruity and more elegant," he explained. "I don't blend wine, I blend fruit. It starts from the vineyards in the summertime, tasting

Above (top): 18 metres beneath the streets of Reims, Henriot's cellars boast a cool, constant 11C.

Above (bottom): Like any self-respecting *Maison de Champagne*, Henriot marks its vineyards in stone.

the berries and trying to find some balance between the villages."

Before long the results were beginning to show through in Henriot NV, which represents 95% of the 1.5 million bottles produced. This is particularly true of the flagship Blanc de Blancs which is carefully constructed each year. Some 70% of the grapes are bought from outside, from growers whose plots express a specific terroir. Collectively, they are the equivalent of a chef's spice rack.

Fresnet later moved to take care of GH Mumm in 2020 but died tragically young three years later, aged just 56. And yet his greatest impact was probably at Henriot where he was responsible for some of its most impressive wines, including the prestige cuvées: Cuvée Hemera and Cuve 38. The latter, launched by Joseph Henriot in 1990, is based on the Grand Cru villages of Oger, Mesnil-sur-Oger, Chouilly and Avize in the Côte des Blancs. The wines are vatted together in a giant stainless-steel tank that holds 467 hectolitres. Every year 15% of the blend is refreshed with new wine and 15% is drawn off as a reserve wine, some of which is bottled as Cuve 38 that boasts an average age of 18 years.

In October 2022 Henriot was acquired by Artémis Domaines, owned by the Pinault family whose wines includes Château Latour in Bordeaux. Two months later the Pinault's gobbled up Jacquesson, only to offload their earlier purchase within a year. Today Henriot is part of the giant Terroirs et Vignerons de Champagne cooperative, which produces France's most popular champagne: Nicolas Feuillatte.

Above: Ripening chardonnay vines destined for Henriot's Brut Souverain NV.

TASTING NOTES

HENRIOT NV BLANC DE BLANCS

Made primarily from Côtes des Blanc fruit, this is a crisp, lively lemon-scented wine with a feint trace of white flowers, possibly honeysuckle, as well. It has more depth and texture than many a Blanc de Blancs.

HENRIOT CUVÉE HEMERA 2013

Henriot's top cuvée is an equal blend of chardonnay and pinot noir from six Grand Cru villages in the Côte des Blancs and the Montagne de Reims. There are aromas of fresh and candied citrus fruit with some toasty notes, with quite a firm, lean structure on the tongue with a lingering, slaty finish.

JACQUESSON
DIZY

Despite its late eighteenth-century roots, Jacquesson has reinvented itself in the mould of a modern champagne grower thanks to the Chiquet brothers who have trimmed back sales in pursuit of quality. Their maverick approach stands out from the corporate world of 'big champagne' driven by the need to grow brands.

In the words of Jean-Hervé Chiquet, the firm bought by his father in 1978 was: "a classic little Champagne House that my brother and I transformed over 30 years into a grower-like operation." He and Laurent Chiquet took over in 1990, which is when it all began to change. "There is no continuity between Jacquesson of the past and Jacquesson now."

For all that, the House was established in 1798 in what is now Châlons-en-Champagne by Memmie Jacquesson and found an early admirer in Napoleon. Sales took off under Memmie's son Adolphe, whose ingenious invention in 1844 of the *muselet* – the little wire cage on every bottle – has held back countless corks from escaping. Five years later, Jacquesson had reached America with a shipment abandoned in San Francisco Bay when the crew deserted to join the gold rush. Bottles unearthed from the mud, 30 years later, had "a very fair flavour" apparently, having "effervesced slightly on uncorking" as Tom Stevenson recalls in his *World Encyclopedia of Champagne and Sparkling Wine.*

From a peak of over a million bottles sold in 1867, Jacquesson went downhill, and by the time it was acquired in 1978 sales were around 450,000 from some 45 hectares of vineyards, of which a third were owned by the House. The House reolocated to the village of Dizy, west of Aÿ and, after 14 years, old man Chiquet handed over the reins to his sons. He was, claimed Jean-Hervé, "fed up with two guys saying the same thing every morning".

"We found that to make good wine you need three things; good terroir, but that's just pure luck to be born in the right place. You need to work hard, that's obvious, but third and very important; you mustn't keep what's not good enough." As a result, Jacquesson now has 29 hectares of its own, plus another 8ha under contract to produce around 250,000 bottles a year. It is about 70% of what a typical Champagne House would produce from that amount of vineyards, thanks partly to lower yields and partly to a refusal to use the second pressing, or taille. The brothers also moved towards organic viticulture, not an easy undertaking in Champagne.

The vineyards lie in the Vallée de la Marne and the Côte des Blancs, half planted with chardonnay, 30% pinot noir and the rest an ever-declining proportion of pinot meunier. Fermentation is carried out in wooden vats to help oxygenate the wine during vinification rather than add oaky flavours to the end result. But what really sets Jacquesson apart is the absence of a House style to reflect each particular year as best it can. As Jean-Hervé put it: "For us the idea of making the same wine

every year would be extremely boring."

This philosophy gave birth to the brothers' one and only blend that started with Cuvée 700. The idea is simply to try and create the best blend possible each year using reserve wines to add complexity rather than achieve consistency. In 2005, with Cuvée 733, they decided to hold back some of the wine and release it much later as a *dégorgement tardif* (late disgorged) bottling. This is something they have done every year since, allowing Jacquesson fans to compare two versions of the same blend, one with around four years' ageing on the lees, the other with around nine. They do make other champagnes including a vintage, but the focus is very much on the Cuvée which represents an antidote to Non-Vintage conformity. "Our approach is essentially selfish," says Jean-Hervé, who goes on to explain his target audience: "Basically we make the wine for the two best customers of Jacquesson – Laurent and I."

It is certainly a maverick approach that has won plenty of fans and been a boost to the whole concept of grower champagne. In 2022, with no family heirs to leave their business to, the Chiquet brothers decided to sell to Artémis Domaines, the wine group owned by the Pinault family, whose portfolio includes Château Latour and, until recently, Champagne Henriot. "We will continue to supply the company with grapes from our own vineyards and I will stay on as a member of the board but without an operational role," says Jean-Hervé.

Opposite (left): After the first pressing in a traditional vertical press, the second pressing or taille is sold on.

Opposite (right): Long ageing on the lees helps imbue Jacquesson with its finesse and complexity.

Right: The Chiquets like to ferment their wines in oak to add oxygen rather than flavour.

TASTING NOTES

CHAMPAGNE JACQUESSON BRUT CUVÉE NO. 746 NV

Based on the 2018 vintage, after a year hit by late frost – especially in the Côte des Blancs – and which finished hot and rainy, the wine required rigorous sorting at harvest-time. The result is a fine balance of elegance and richness – very quaffable and refreshing.

JACQUESSON CUVÉE 742 DEGORGEMENT TARDIF

The number translates as 2014, a year when the grapes ripened beautifully after a cool, wet July and August. It is principally chardonnay from Aÿ, Dizy and Hautvillers, and disgorged in 2023 to give a mix of orchard fruits and citrus zest, with Jacquesson's typically saline, mineral texture.

JOSEPH PERRIER
CHÂLONS-EN-CHAMPAGNE

Still family-owned, and one of the original Grandes Marques, Joseph Perrier has been referred to as 'the other Perrier' – apparently it's not an uncommon name in these parts. Being the only leading Champagne House in Châlons-en-Champagne sets it apart from the crowd in Reims and Épernay.

The firm's roots go back to Perrier Fils, who were wine merchants in what was then Châlons-sur-Marne at the start of the nineteenth century. One branch of the family, headed by Pierre-Nicolas Perrier, moved to Épernay and established Perrier-Jouët in 1811. Fourteen years later in 1825, his nephew Joseph Perrier set up in Châlons, then a key champagne town with 13 Houses of good repute. Today it is the sole survivor.

In the 1880s Joseph's grandson, Gabriel Perrier, sold out to Paul Pithois, another local wine merchant, whose great-great grandson Benjamin Fourmon is now in charge. The name never changed because Joseph Perrier was well established in France and the West Indies, as it was in India and the UK by the time of its sale. Customers included Queen Victoria and Edward Prince of Wales. A letter from St James' Palace in 1889, requested a dosage of '2.5%', which, while not Brut, equates to a relatively dry 'Sec'.

Pithois had a holiday home in the village of Cumières on the banks of the Marne, where he acquired nine hectares of vineyards, and in neighbouring Hautvillers and Daméry, which the family still own. He was also the first secretary of the Syndicat du Marques du Champagne, and was involved with the great French scientist, Louis Pasteur.

Châlons was largely unscathed by the First World War, and the firm was happy to help the Krug family store their wine in its cellars while the German artillery pulverised Reims. Joseph Perrier survived the lean, inter-war years and the wave of buy-ups after the war. During the 1960s, as the Marne valley transitioned from fruit farming to vines, the family acquired more south-facing vineyards around Verneuil, and today own 23 hectares. Meanwhile, another family member, a dashing French army colonel who spoke impeccable English, helped develop the UK market.

Like many such Houses, Joseph Perrier found itself with a lengthening tail of smaller shareholders which made it vulnerable to a predatory bid from one of the big players. Jean-Claude Fourmon, who took over in 1979, turned to his first cousin Alain Thiénot, who, with his own House and later Canard-Duchêne, was becoming a major force in Champagne. He managed to buy up the shares, including a stake owned by Laurent-Perrier, and keep Joseph Perrier in that select band of family-owned Houses like Pol Roger and Roederer.

A few years later the town of Châlons swapped its suffix from 'sur-Marne' to 'en-Champagne', much to the family's delight. "That made

Épernay and Reims so jealous!" cried Jean-Claude with glee. "Now we can have 'champagne' twice on our labels." His son Benjamin succeeded as Perrier's president in 2019 when its *chef de cave* Nathalie Laplaige was crowned 'cellar master of the year' in the annual Trophées Champenoise.

The vineyards lean towards pinot noir and pinot meunier, though the core wine, the Cuvée Royal NV Brut, includes an equal share of chardonnay in the blend. It comes with a distinctive pale lemon-yellow label in contrast to the deep egg-yolk of Veuve Clicquot, and accounts for at least three-quarters of sales. Above sits the Vintage Brut Cuvée and Cuvée Josephine, a majestic 60:40 marriage of chardonnay and pinot noir.

These have been joined by a trio of special cuvées based on the three champagne grapes to show off the different varieties and Joseph Perrier's grower credentials. Each are from small, individual plots, from a single vintage and are all *Brut Nature*. Among them is a pinot noir from La Côte à Bras in Cumières, and a pinot meunier from Verneil.

Once the grapes are crushed in presses near the vineyards, the juice is transported to Châlons, a good half an hour away. The winery is an old townhouse and boasts some spectacular Gallo-Roman cellars cut horizontally into the side of a small hill some 2,000 years ago. They were extended to three kilometres in the mid-nineteenth century, when shafts were sunk into the hillside for ventilation and natural light. A further two kilometres of cellars next-door have been added and connected by a tunnel, while more vineyards have been acquired in Vitryat and Cumières. And in 2020, the House finally threw open its doors to the public with a brand-new visitor centre.

Opposite: An autumnal view of some of Joseph Perrier's vineyards on the banks of the River Marne, near the Premier Cru village of Cumières.

Right: An Art Deco poster for the brand from the 1920s by J Stall (1874–1933).

TASTING NOTES

JOSEPH PERRIER CUVÉE ROYALE BRUT NV

The other 'yellow label' to Veuve Clicquot's, Cuvée Royale is an ethereal, light, classic apéritif-style champagne made from an equal blend of the three grapes sourced from 20 villages including Cumières, Damery and Hautvillers. There's a whiff of pear on the nose, a supple texture and a lively, fresh finish.

JOSEPH PERRIER LA CÔTE À BRAS AH83

The code refers to a single parcel in the premier cru village of Cumières. It is pure pinot noir and gloriously fruity on the nose with lemon zest and mandarin. It seems to firm up on the tongue with its flinty, mineral undercurrent that keeps the fruit in check – long and faintly spicy on the finish.

KRUG
REIMS

Whether Krug is the world's greatest champagne is obviously a matter of opinion, but it's clearly what the *chef de cave*, Julie Cavil, and her team aspire to every year when they release Krug Grande Cuvée. The attention to detail is awesome, as is the price.

"With Krug there is no hierarchy," says sixth-generation director Olivier Krug, and by that he means its famed multi-vintage Grande Cuvée is made to be the equal of vintage Krug with as much care taken in its production. Also, unlike other Houses, there is no cheaper NV version to give a glimpse of greatness. Priced up to £200 a bottle, Grande Cuvée occupies a rarefied niche and there's not much of it. Krug's total production is less than 0.2% of champagne, which puts it below 625,000 bottles a year.

The story starts in 1834, when Joseph Krug, an ambitious young German, began working for the leading House at the time: Champagne Jacquesson in Châlons-sur-Marne. Before long he was co-managing the business and married to his partner's English sister-in-law, Emma Anne Jaunay. Instead of cruising into a comfortable retirement, he departed to set up his own business in Reims in 1843. He had the backing of a local wine merchant, for whom he had been blending wine on the side.

The art of blending was the key to quality, in his view, a vision he expressed in a small red notebook in 1848. "Joseph wrote that if you want to make a great wine you need good elements from good origins," says Olivier. The latter referred to the terroir, while the 'elements' were the base wines that made up the blend. Some would have been produced years earlier and held back as reserve wines, which gave him the means to circumvent the vagaries of one growing season to the next, and produce a top champagne every year.

On his death in 1866, his son Paul took over. The wine was already selling as far afield as St Petersburg, New York and Rio de Janeiro, and being half-English, Paul helped to establish the champagne across the Channel. In the 1880s Paul Krug bought the first vineyards – 20 hectares around Mailly on the Montagne de Reims, but then sold them to focus on what he felt the family did best: blending.

While the name 'Grande Cuvée' is more recent, each release seeks to be what it calls 'the most generous expression of champagne' in keeping with the vision of its founder. Well over a hundred different plots are individually tended and harvested, and then made into separate wines. These are then blended with reserve wines from vintages stretching back up to 20 years from its final release date.

The first fermentation is in oak barrels and with the years ageing on the lees followed by up to a year after disgorgement, the wine's greatest ingredient may well be time. And the House's greatest asset might be its unrivalled library of reserve wines and the skill of its *chef de cave* to marry them in the best possible way. The specific composition of every bottle can be discovered using the Krug ID; six digits on the back of the bottle.

In the early 1970s Krug finally acquired vineyards of its own, including Clos du Mesnil, a tiny walled vineyard of 1.9 hectares in the village of Mesnil-sur-Oger that was originally planted by Benedictine monks at the end of the seventeenth century. The purchase of what has become arguably the greatest single vineyard champagne of all involved a partnership with the Cognac House Rémy Martin, which in turn led to Krug's sale to LVMH in 1999.

Below (left): After nine years of honing his craft with Champagne Jacquesson in Châlons-sur-Marne, Johann-Josef Krug founded a House of his own in 1843.

Below (right): The founder's leather-bound journal in which he recorded his notes and observations on the art of blending champagne.

Opposite (left): A prime piece of Champagne real estate – the fabled walled vineyard of Clos du Mesnil in the village of Mesnil-sur-Oger, which Krug acquired in the early 1970s.

Opposite (right): A grand old bottle of Krug with its imperial crest. Note the word 'Sec', signifying a dosage of more than 17 grams/litre of sugar which, by today's standards, would be anything but 'dry'.

Krug happily admits it sold more bottles at the end of the nineteenth century than it does today, and its diminutive size allows it to fly beneath the radar of its corporate owners and carry on much as before. What LVMH has done is invest in a striking new winery for Krug called 'Joseph 2.0' in the Grand Cru village of Ambonnay, 30 kilometres south of Reims, where it had been made in the same building for 160 years. After the constraints of winemaking in the city, Krug is now produced amidst the vines in what resembles an upturned boat with a copper-bottomed hull. Its first wines from Ambonnay won't see the light of day until 2031.

TASTING NOTES

KRUG GRANDE CUVÉE BRUT NV

Krug's pride and joy is a moveable feast of grape varieties from up to 200 carefully selected plots, with reserve wines accounting for up to half the blend. The result is a firm, rich, golden champagne with some mellow dried fruits at its core, a fine mousse and a toasty, nutty aroma.

KRUG VINTAGE 2006

With soaring temperatures and bursts of intense rain, 2006 was a challenging year. In a blend of roughly half pinot noir and a third chardonnay, and aged for over ten years, this is a generous, almost decadent wine. Notably aromatic with scents of citrus peel, meringue and sugared almonds.

LANSON
REIMS

There was certainly an element of tragedy in the rise and fall of the great Maison Lanson during the 1990s. But since 2006 it has been under new ownership as part of the independent Lanson-BCC group, and is determined to take on Moët & Chandon and Veuve Clicquot and win.

It began with a marriage between François Delamotte of Reims, who owned a fairly sizeable vineyard in Cumières in the Marne valley, and Marie-Claude Thérèse de Bourgogne, whose father had a vineyard in Aÿ. The combined holding encouraged François to set up his own Champagne House in 1760. Some 40 years later, his youngest son, Nicolas-Louis, took over and, as a newly decorated Knight of the Order of Malta, decided to use the famous Maltese cross as the emblem of his champagne.

The Lansons didn't arrive on the scene until 1837, when Jean-Baptiste Lanson, an old friend of the family, became a director and eventually succeeded as sole owner of the firm. It changed its name to Lanson Père & Fils and under Jean-Baptiste's son, Victor-Marie Lanson, sales began to take off, especially in the UK where it was distributed by the well-established London merchants Percy Fox. In 1900 it won a converted new customer in Queen Victoria, and has held a royal warrant ever since.

Lanson's real growth began in the late 1920s, when it acquired some superb cellars and land on the Rue de Courlancy in the heart of Reims. In charge was the formidable figure of Victor Lanson, who travelled widely selling to everyone from Indian maharajas to gold miners who had struck it rich in Australia. Meanwhile he began a serious expansion of the family's vineyards in Champagne, eventually reaching 208 hectares.

Lanson had been making a rosé as early as 1833 and became one of the first big Houses to develop the market for pink champagne under Victor. To produce it, he was buying pinot noir from the Aube, and this was also the key grape in Lanson Black Label that first appeared in 1938. Whether he was inspired by a certain Johnnie Walker, the name has always been in English, even in France. "I only make champagne for myself. What I can't drink I sell," Victor used to claim, and as a man who reputedly averaged three bottles a day, it wasn't such an idle boast.

As the Lanson family grew, so did the number of private shareholders and outside investors which created the potential for lots of infighting. During the 1970s the Gardinière family, in-laws of the Lanson's who had made a fortune flogging fertilisers in America, steadily acquired all the shares. In 1984 they sold out to the BSN group, with sixth-generation Jean-Baptiste Lanson still in charge. He insisted it was better for the champagne to be part of a large, professional group than a vast, squabbling family, but things took a turn for the worse.

Thanks to Black Label, Lanson was selling up to 10 million bottles a year and was second only to Moët & Chandon when the First Gulf War kicked off in August 1990. The subsequent oil crisis helped crash the champagne market and LVMH seized its chance the following year. It wasn't interested in the brand, or the company's headquarters in Reims, so much as those lovely vineyards. This became clear when Lanson was quickly sold to the giant Marne et Champagne group, who acquired the brand, the company HQ, the cellars and four years of stocks, but not a single vine. Astonishingly they paid the same amount for which it and its vineyards had been sold six months earlier.

Given the eye-watering prices of a good vineyard nowadays, it was a spectacular deal for the owners of Moët & Chandon, who almost crippled their closest rival in the process. However, Lanson has bounced back, acquiring a pilot vineyard – the Malmaison estate in 2010. Today it owns 60 hectares, with a close relationship with growers from a further 360 ha that supply the rest of its needs.

All the while Lanson has long been a sponsor of Wimbledon, where some 150,000 glasses of Black Label are drunk during the fortnight, depending on the weather. Maybe an English sparkler is plotting to replace it, but for now Lanson appears safe on Centre Court.

Black Label is now officially 'Le Black Creation' with a number signifying the base vintage to which older reserve wines are added. The aim is to "talk much more precisely to all the critics and sommeliers about what is in the blend each year," explained Lanson's president François Van Aal. Whether consumers care is something else.

Opposite: In the heart of Reims, with the city's cathedral in the background, pickers set to work on the one-hectare walled vineyard of Clos Lanson. In 2016, Lanson announced it would be using the grapes to produce a single vineyard cuvée.

Above (left): Clos Lanson is a Blanc de Blancs, fermented in oak barrels and left on its lees for eight years. On average, only 8,000 bottles will be produced.

Above (right): A classic *pupitre* in the Lanson cellar.

TASTING NOTES

LANSON LE BLACK CRÉATION

Le Black Création is not so dissimilar to the old Black Label, with its light core of pinot noir fruit and trace of lemon syllabub on the tongue, and its muted aroma of spring flowers. The number on the label refers to the base vintage, and thus suggests some variation from year to year – that's the theory.

LANSON NOBLE CHAMPAGNE 2005

This is a pure Grand Cru blend of Montagne de Reims pinot noir and Côte des Blancs chardonnay that slumbered for almost two decades in Lanson's cellars. It offers a fine mousse, with plenty of pastry and baked apple notes, yet an invigorating freshness for all its years on the lees.

LAURENT-PERRIER
TOURS-SUR-MARNE

Now into its third century, Laurent-Perrier was a very small brand before the Second World War. Its renaissance since then to become one of the big beasts of champagne was down to one man above all: the legendary Bernard de Nonancourt.

On 4 May 1945, de Nonancourt, then a young tank commander, found himself in the Bavarian Alps beneath Hitler's secret mountain hideaway, the Eagle's Nest – as recalled in *Wine & War*, by Don and Petie Kladstrup. Because he was from Champagne and knew something about wine, he was ordered to investigate a cave beneath the summit, believed to contain the Führer's personal cellar. Having dynamited the steel door, de Nonancourt squeezed in to discover an incredible stash of wine. Amidst the Châteaux Lafite, Margaux and d'Yquem were hundreds of cases of Salon. Some 44 years later, he was to add this glittering, boutique brand to his Laurent-Perrier empire.

Founded in 1812 in Tours-sur-Marne by André-Michel Pierlot, the House was named after the cellar master Eugène Laurent, who inherited the business only to die accidentally in 1887, leaving his wife in charge. Mathilde Emilie Perrier was another of those redoubtable champagne widows who began to build what was now Laurent-Perrier. She pioneered a *sans-sucre* version for the UK market with the strapline: "The champagne recommended when others are prohibited." It was resurrected as Laurent-Perrier Ultra Brut in 1981.

On the eve of the First World War, Laurent-Perrier's cellars held a respectable 600,000 bottles. By 1939, after the devastation of the war

Opposite: A vintage French postcard featuring a group of people packing crates and baskets of Laurent-Perrier champagne in Epernay, circa 1910.

Above: With only 110 hectares in Champagne, Laurent-Perrier is hardly self-sufficient in grapes. But Bernard de Nonancourt always maintained it was better to have contracts with good growers than own poor vineyards.

Right: Laurent-Perrier was one of the pioneers of bone dry champagne with its 'Sans-Sucre' label in the UK in the late nineteenth century.

and the Depression, that number had shrunk to just 36,000. Its new owner, Marie-Louise Lanson de Nonancourt, bricked up the cellar, installed a statue of the Virgin Mary and waited for her sons to return. The eldest, Maurice, died in a concentration camp, so it was left to Bernard to rebuild Laurent-Perrier.

His mother insisted he had a thorough apprenticeship in all aspects of production at her family's Champagne House, Lanson, until she was satisfied he was serious. In 1948 he took over a business with 20 staff and sales of 80,000 bottles a year and built it into what is now the largest independent family House. With his cellar master Edouard Leclerc and then Alain Terrier, he developed the fresh, elegant House style with chardonnay accounting for half the NV Brut, and the use of a special strain of yeast to enhance the fruit over any bread-like aromas. The House was a pioneer in using temperature-controlled stainless-steel fermentation tanks.

Another early innovation was a rosé in 1968, when the colour pink was considered frivolous in the extreme by any serious Champagne House. The method chosen was that of a still wine like a Provençal rosé, where the colour bleeds in from the skins of black grapes, in this case pinot noir, and not by blending in a drop of red wine which is standard practice here. The amount of skin contact is down to "the aromas the cellar master is looking for, in terms of fresh fruit, of raspberries and strawberries," explains Adam Guy, MD of Laurent-Perrier UK.

With just over 130 hectares, enough to supply a tenth of its needs, Laurent-Perrier is reliant on its long-term contracts with good growers, but has never felt constrained by this. "One of the reasons Bernard was

able to grow the House so much in the twentieth century is because he was the only MD and owner who was in the vineyards spending time with the growers," says Guy.

De Nonancourt believed the real art lay in the blend, as exemplified by Grand Siècle, first released in 1959 as a marriage of the '52, '53 and '55 vintage. Bottled in a replica champagne bottle from Versailles at the time of Louis XIV, the Sun King, it has nearly always been a trio of top years. "It's about attempting to recreate the perfect year," says Guy. "The year that nature will never give you."

Grand Siècle now has a second wine – Héritage, and both are looked after by de Nonancourt's grand-daughter, Lucy, whose mother and aunt are also both actively involved in the business. As for Bernard himself, "he was a gentle giant of a man," recalls David Hesketh, the previous MD of Laurent-Perrier UK. "You saw his passion for champagne, and it must have been amazing to have worked alongside him in the days he was building the House to what it is now."

Opposite: Château de Louvois, home of the House's Prestige Cuvée, Grand Siècle, just outside Tours-sur-Marne.

Above: Laurent-Perrier's iconic label.

TASTING NOTES

LAURENT-PERRIER BLANC DE BLANCS BRUT NATURE NV

Thanks to global warming and the skill of the blending team, you would be hard pressed to guess that this was zero dosage. It is dry, but not bone dry, and the fine mousse and delicate silky texture help round out the fruit and give it a little more depth on the tongue before it slips away.

LAURENT-PERRIER 1812 HÉRITAGE BRUT

This is a blend of chardonnay and pinot noir, with the former just in front, that is carefully constructed from the reserve wines in Laurent-Perrier's cellars. There are white fruits and the scent of baked apples that come through on the palate in this elegant, finely tuned champagne.

MOËT & CHANDON
ÉPERNAY

Somebody somewhere is cracking open a bottle of Moët & Chandon every six seconds, it is popularly acclaimed. Precisely how much is sold is kept secret, but sales of its Moët Impérial Brut NV must be close to 30 million bottles a year. That's an awful lot of bubbles.

Moët is nothing if not imperial. It is the flagship fizz of the mighty LVMH Moët Hennessy Louis Vuitton, which dominates the champagne trade. It also links directly to the Emperor himself since Napoleon was a lifelong customer and then friend of Jean-Rémy Moët. The House was founded by his grandfather, Claude Moët, in 1743 and had supplied the court of Versailles when the champagne-loving Madame de Pompadour was Louis XV's favourite.

Jean-Rémy Moët took over in 1792, when the French were revolting. The wine survived any guilt by association with the *Ancien Régime*, and by 1801 Jean-Rémy was supplying Napoleon and Josephine.

Napoleon would stock up with champagne whenever passing through on his next military campaign. In 1814 Jean-Rémy was awarded the *Légion d'Honneur* for organising the defence and resistance of Épernay against the Cossacks, scouts of the Russian troops, thus allowing Napoleon to reach Épernay before the Allied armies. He also opened his cellars in order to preserve his neighbour's properties.

Jean-Rémy's son-in-law, Pierre-Gabriel Chandon de Briailles, became a partner and the firm was renamed Moët & Chandon in 1833. Some years earlier, Pierre-Gabriel had bought the ruined Abbey of Hautvillers and its vineyards. By the turn of the century, visitors would gasp at the industrial scale of Moët's champagne factory in Épernay with its 1,500 workers. George Kessler, the firm's US agent, boasted record imports of 102,000 cases in 1902 – more than a quarter of Moët's worldwide sales. Kessler was famed for his lavish parties in New York and London, and once flooded the Savoy's courtyard to create a Venetian lagoon stocked with live swans, ducks and sea trout. Enrico Caruso serenaded guests as they guzzled champagne aboard a giant gondola. The evening ended with a baby elephant bearing an enormous cake.

From this peak of conspicuous consumption, the brand slipped into decline until Comte Robert-Jean de Vogüé entered the company in 1932 and soon took over. He proved a dynamic and inspirational leader for Moët & Chandon and champagne in general. Vogüé was bold enough to launch the luxurious prestige cuvée Dom Pérignon in 1936 despite the economic gloom, and represented the industry during the war, dealing

with Hitler's *weinführer*, Otto Klaebisch. He also negotiated a substantial increase in grape prices to help the growers and champagne's long-term sustainability.

Vogüé seemed to have an innate gift for marketing, and he understood how to use public relations and celebrity endorsement long before many in the region. Maurice Chevalier, once the highest-paid star in Hollywood, was courted to sprinkle some stardust on his brands. Before long it wasn't just Moët and Dom Pérignon, as the company acquired first Mercier in 1970, Ruinart in 1973, and also Parfums Christian Dior in 1971. Today LVMH controls around one-fifth of all champagne and

Opposite: Château de Saran, built in 1801 near the village of Chouilly by Jean-Rémy Moët, is where the House now entertains its top clients and guests.

Left: Third-generation Jean-Rémy Moët took over in 1792, and built the foundations of the most powerful Champagne House of all, with a little help from his lifelong friend – Napoleon Bonaparte.

Above: Bottles lie *sur lattes* in Moët's cellars, slowly transforming into champagne. The firm's cellars are the largest in the region, stretching for 17 miles beneath the streets of Épernay.

Should the power
of the press be limited?
Moët & Chandon think so.
Our manager Monsieur Philippe Saunier continues to use our great wooden presses.
By carefully controlling their pressure we can ensure no colour from the grape skins
finds its way into the juice. Just as we have since 1743.
MOËT
MOËT & CHANDON
MOËT & CHANDON
The world's most famous champagne.

MOËT
MOËT & CHANDON
A cellarman at Moët & Chandon together
with the tools of his trade. His hands.
The perfect clarity of
Moët & Chandon is only
achieved by delicate
manipulation of the bottle.
Originally this painstaking
task was performed by
hand. Thanks to men like
Christian Niellez it still is.
MOËT & CHANDON
The world's most famous champagne.

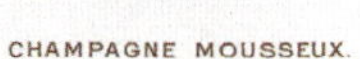

SILLERY MOUSSEUX SUPÉRIEUR.

CRÉMANT D'AY, ROSÉ.

GRAND CRÉMANT IMPÉRIAL.

WHITE STAR (SEC).

BRUT IMPÉRIAL (EXTRA SEC).

some two-thirds of the US market.

"We like to say 'bigger is better'," was how its former marketing director, Arnaud de Saignes, referred to the firm's 1,180 hectares of vineyards that supply over one-third of Moët's needs. Benoît Gouez, its respected *chef de cave*, insists that quality and quantity are not mutually exclusive in champagne. LVMH inspires respect among rivals, given the group's continued success and growth.

Vast sales of its Imperial Brut NV has made Moët & Chandon the world's most valuable wine brand. Less well-known are its vintage expressions, which now include the Grand Vintage Collection which is kept on its lees – the natural sediment in the bottle, for around 15 years before being finally disgorged. The aim is to ensure maximum ageing potential.

Opposite: There's plenty of Art Deco nostalgia in this UK ad campaign from the 1970s.

Above: Within Moët's early range, White Star was sold as a demi-sec with 20g/l of sugar in the American market until it was withdrawn in 2012.

TASTING NOTES

MOËT & CHANDON IMPERIAL BRUT NV

The flagship of Moët & Chandon since 1869, Brut Imperial is renowned the world over for its complexity and consistency. Golden straw yellow in colour with green highlights, it is characterised by a bright fruitiness, a richly flavourful palate and an elegant maturity, that continually seduce and delight.

MOËT & CHANDON VINTAGE 2016

Roughly half chardonnay and a third pinot noir, with the balance made up of pinot meunier, this expression of a none-too-easy year in Champagne has a bready, cake-like aroma with some soft red fruits coming through underneath. Silky-textured and lingering as it slips away.

G.H. MUMM
REIMS

With its cuddly brand name, and easily recognisable label, Mumm Cordon Rouge has been a top-selling champagne since the 1900s, when it graced hotel bars in New Zealand to the brothels of New Orleans. It is now a stablemate of Perrier-Jouët under Pernod Ricard.

"Wine flowed much more than water did during those periods," recalled the jazz legend Jelly Roll Morton in the 1930s about New Orleans at the turn of the century. "The kind of wine I'm speaking about, I don't mean sauternes or nothing like that, I mean champagne … among the main ones were Clicquot, which is a French wine, and Mumm's Extra Dry … that was an English wine."

While Morton may have muddled the origins, he was right about the names. Mumm was a massive brand thanks to its flagship Cordon Rouge, launched by Georges Hermann von Mumm in 1876. With its eye-catching red sash label, as though awarded the Légion d'Honneur, it was distinctive and easy to remember. It flowed through every whorehouse and jazz joint on New Orleans Basin Street, and by 1902 it was selling more than one million cases in the States. Global sales were over three million cases, almost one-tenth of champagne's total.

The firm was established in Reims in 1827 by Georges Hermann's father and two uncles, who had crossed from the Rhineland where the Mumms were well-established wine merchants and vineyard owners. The family began buying plots in Champagne, starting with Verzenay in 1840, where they were one of the first to instal a press house beside the vineyards to crush the grapes before they lost freshness. For what they bought in from the growers, they preferred grapes rather than fermented wine, like most of their rivals.

By 1913, G. H. Mumm owned around 50 hectares, mainly in the Côte des Blancs. Unfortunately the owners had failed to take out French citizenship like the other Houses of German origin, and the whole company was confiscated by the state on the outbreak of war. In 1920 it was sold at auction to a consortium that included the Dubonnets, whose son-in-law, René Lalou, was appointed a director. As a young Parisian lawyer, he knew nothing of the champagne trade, but he learnt fast. He built on the salesmanship of Georges Hermann in the late nineteenth century and became the driving force behind the brand for almost 50 years.

Below (left): The headquarters of G.H. Mumm & Cie in Reims – the House founded by a family of German winemakers from the Rhineland in 1827.

Below (middle): The Moulin de Verzenay, a famous landmark by the Grand Cru village of Verzenay, in the Montagne de Reims, overlooks some of Mumm's 218 hectares of vineyards.

Below (right): Second-generation Georges Hermann Mumm was responsible for launching Cordon Rouge, with its distinctive red sash label, in 1876. By the end of the century global sales were topping three million bottles.

The original Mumms didn't quite give up on their brand, and briefly requisitioned it during the Second World War. René Lalou was soon back in charge, however, and being an avid art collector, commissioned the Japanese artist Léonard Foujita to design the rose on the top of Mumm's new rosé champagne, launched in 1957. By then Seagram, the giant US spirits producer, had begun to buy into the brand, followed by Perrier-Jouët and Heidsieck Monopole. Before long they controlled Mumm outright, and this gave it a hefty boost in distribution. In the UK it was almost always on promotion through the Oddbins off-license that Seagram owned.

Cordon Rouge was famed for its fresh, floral, easy-going style with a lightness that belied its dominant grape – pinot noir. The variety accounts for almost 80% of the 218 hectares owned by Mumm, 160 of them in eight Grand Cru villages including Aÿ, Bouzy, Verzenay and Cramant. The special Cuvée René Lalou, a 50:50 blend of pinot noir and chardonnay from these villages, was first released in the 1960s, only to be dropped before Seagram sold the business. Since 2006 Mumm has been back in French hands, alongside Perrier-Jouët, under Pernod Ricard.

In the meantime, the old Lalou-inspired cuvée has been reinstated, and with its spicy, fulsome, almost buttery style, it is quite different to Mumm's main expression, and is now part of the RSRV range of four cuvées entirely from Grand Cru vineyards. Cordon Rouge went through a lean patch in the late twentieth century and some pesky British journalists declared its Californian offshoot Mumm Cuvée Napa was better in blind tastings, despite being half the price. They were told, with wonderful Gallic distain, not to compare blondes with brunettes.

Today's Mumm Cordon Rouge is infinitely better. Recent PR stunts have included Cordon Rouge Stellar for drinking in space, but rather more serious has been a commitment to ship its wines to the US under sail to reduce carbon emissions. A first shipment reached New York in 2024.

Above: A poster from the 1930s for Mumm's flagship brand. Note the none-too-subtle nod to a certain popular brand of soft drink.

TASTING NOTES

MUMM CORDON ROUGE BRUT NV

Hugely popular in France, Cordon Rouge accounts for around 90% of Mumm's production. With a well-judged dosage of 9g/l, compared to around 12g in the past, it has a nervy freshness to balance the soft texture of its predominantly black fruit with the blend 45% pinot noir and 25% pinot meunier.

MUMM CUVÉE R. LALOU 2008

This special cuvée, only released in top years, is an equal blend of chardonnay and pinot noir from 12 carefully chosen Grand Cru vineyards. Aged on its lees for over ten years, there is a real depth and roundness to the palate with buttery, pastry notes giving way to a long, elegant finish.

PERRIER-JOUËT
ÉPERNAY

The swirling imagery around Perrier-Jouët and the beautiful enamelled Belle Époque bottles dates from the height of the art nouveau movement in Paris. The design encapsulates the flowery elegance of the wine, yet it took until the late 1960s for it to finally appear in public.

For Pierre Bezukhov, in Tolstoy's *War and Peace*, the Great Comet of 1811 was a bad omen, perhaps signalling the end of the world. But for newlyweds Pierre-Nicolas Perrier and Rose-Adélaïde Jouët, it was a symbol of hope for the champagne business they had just founded. This feeling was reinforced by that year's exceptional vintage.

Demand for it allowed the couple to buy premises at the prosaic-sounding 24 Rue du Commerce in Épernay. By the end of the century, such was Perrier-Jouët's popularity, it had moved to the Avenue de Champagne, the smartest street in town. The man who really built the brand was their son, Charles Perrier, who took over in 1848. He was also mayor of Épernay and a member of parliament.

By the 1850s he was wealthy enough to commission the imposing Château Perrier across the street from his HQ where he could entertain Napoleon III and his wife, the Empress Eugénie. The first bottles of Perrier-Jouët arrived in England as early as 1815, just months after the Battle of Waterloo, while shipments to America followed in 1837.

A decade later, the firm's UK agent tried to pioneer bone-dry champagne with a *Zéro Dosage* bottling, but without success. The English fashion for Brut only really started in the 1870s, by which point Perrier-Jouët was in great demand across the Channel, with Britain soon accounting for 90% of sales. Among its fans were Queen Victoria, Edward the Prince of Wales, Oscar Wilde and 'the most famous actress the world has ever known'. This was the French star of stage and silent screen Sarah Bernhardt, who liked to bathe in Perrier-Jouët, or so it was claimed.

Charles Perrier died in 1878, leaving a thriving business to his nephew, Henri Gallice. The Franco-Prussian War had ended and Europe entered a sustained period of peace and prosperity that was looked back on with deep nostalgia after the horrors of the First World War. Culture and the arts flourished, especially in Paris, where the era became known as the Belle Époque. Its spirit was captured in a beautifully decorated bottle of the same name.

It was in 1902 that Émile Gallé, a master glassmaker and leading light in the Art Nouveau movement, was approached by Henri Gallice to design a bottle for his vintage champagne. The artist was also a renowned botanist and chose a spray of white Japanese anemones from his garden, apparently to reflect the colour and floral nature of chardonnay. Unfortunately there was no way to replicate Gallé's art

Top: Rose Adélaïde-Jouët (top) and her husband Pierre-Nicolas Perrier (below), co-founded the House in 1811, the year of the Great Comet, which proved to be an auspicious omen. But, in reality, it was their son Charles Perrier who built the brand and the family's reputation.

Above: Like Moët & Chandon and Pol Roger, Perrier-Jouët is another grand resident of Épernay's smartest street – the Avenue de Champagne.

Opposite: Belle Époque bottles, in all their glory, resting in the cellars of Perrier-Jouët. The original Art Nouveau design from 1902 could not be reproduced on any scale, and was not publicly released until 1969.

on any scale and the idea was abandoned. It was not until the *chef de cave*, André Bavaret, discovered the original bottles in a cupboard in the 1960s that it was decided to copy the designs and launch the Belle Époque vintage cuvée in 1969 to celebrate Duke Ellington's 70th birthday in Paris. Some 500 privileged customers were given a numbered magnum each, and the rest were sold through Maxim's and Fauchon, the city's swankiest food store. In time Belle Époque was followed by a rosé and a Blanc de Blancs.

By now the House was run by a family cousin Michel Budin, though ownership had passed to Seagram, who also owned Champagne Mumm. This boosted PJ's distribution, especially in the US where "hardly an episode of *Dallas* goes by without JR Ewing knocking back a bottle," wrote Don Hewitson in *The Glory of Champagne*.

Seagram's drinks empire was broken up and Perrier-Jouët found itself passed around until finally settling with Pernod-Ricard in 2006. It is back in French hands, albeit those of a drinks giant best known for spirits like Chivas Regal, Jameson's and Absolut. A few years later, an über-premium Blanc de Blancs from a Grand Cru single vineyard in Cramant was added, priced at a breathtaking £35,000 a case. But you did get to choose the *dosage* to make it bespoke.

Today Perrier-Jouët owns 65 hectares of vineyards, more than half in the Côte des Blancs – enough to supply a quarter of its needs. Hervé Deschamps, its long-serving *chef de caves*, explains how the blending for its Belle Epoque wines, which are always a vintage, is focussed on chardonnay, which he calls the "finest and most delicate of grapes" in Champagne.

TASTING NOTES

PERRIER-JOUËT GRAND BRUT

With its simple gold label, Grand Brut may lack the exuberant exterior of Belle Epoque, but offers a supple well-balanced champagne on the inside. Its flowery scent has a trace of vanilla and puff pastry, while it is ethereal and light on the tongue, finishing a little short.

PERRIER-JOUËT BELLE EPOQUE

There is a real floral elegance to Belle Epoque and some subtle toasty aromas that come through on the palate. Quite whether those aromatic notes of jasmine and honeysuckle that people tend to find in this wine are influenced by the bottle is hard to say. Taste it blind and decide for yourself.

PHILIPPONNAT
MAREUIL-SUR-AŸ

The Philipponnats have been growers and négociants in champagne for almost five centuries, though it is only in the past 50 years that the brand has soared, thanks to its famous single vineyard champagne. It may be corporately owned, but it feels every inch a family-run House.

Charles Philipponnat certainly has pedigree when it comes to champagne. As CEO of the eponymous House, he can trace his family's roots back to 1522, when an ancestor gave up his military career as a Swiss mercenary captain and settled in Aÿ with his own vineyards. By the end of the following century his descendants were supplying red wine to the court of the Sun King, Louis XIV. Quite when they began making sparkling wine is unclear.

The Philipponnats never moved, except to the neighbouring village of Mareuil-sur-Aÿ in 1910. Twenty-five years later, Charles' great uncle bought 5.5 hectares of semi-abandoned vineyards that had been part of the former cellars of the Château de Mareuil, and whose owners had gone bankrupt. If this steep, south-facing plot, surrounded by walls as though it were in Burgundy, was in any way famous, it was because of an old postcard photograph. It showed the vineyards reflected in the Marne canal to resemble a champagne bottle lying on its side.

This was Les Clos des Goisses, which has become home to arguably the most highly regarded single vineyard champagne of them all. "Only about a third was in production, as no-one wanted to break their backs cultivating it," says Charles explaining how his great uncle was able to buy it for a relatively modest sum. A Clos des Goisses champagne was soon released, but it was only when the worn-out vines were replanted with pinot noir in 1964 that the true potential began to emerge.

Positioned to soak up as much sunshine as possible with the angle of the slope as much as 45° in parts, temperatures in this sheltered vineyard are 1.5°C higher than the regional average. This appears to suit the Burgundian black grape perfectly with Clos de Goisses' two-thirds pinot noir and one-third chardonnay. Its ripeness is just what Charles Philipponnat desires. "I believe quality in Champagne is about ripe grapes," he says. "It's about good fruit that you can eat."

He accepts global warming as a reality, but sees it as a positive for Champagne. "I think with Clos des Goisses we have proof that we can grow riper grapes and still make very good wine," he says. "I believe temperature is only one element of terroir, and not the main one, which is soil. If champagne has any problem today, it's with unripeness." The grapes are picked at the peak of physiological ripeness which means the juice is relatively low in acidity. Yet, somehow, the chalky soil and the lack of malolactic fermentation in the cellar helps what little acidity there is to shine through, especially given the wine's low *dosage*. Clos des Goisses has been Extra-Brut for more than 20 years.

But for the chardonnay found here, Philipponnat's other vineyards are all planted with pinot noir which thrives on the south-facing slopes around Aÿ in the heart of Champagne where the Vallée de la Marne, the Montagne de Reims and the Côte des Blancs converge.

In total the House owns 17 hectares and cultivates another five,

accounting for one-third of its needs for a production of around 700,000 bottles. "We buy our grapes mostly from around here," says Charles, who describes the House style as follows: "It's about intensity of flavour and fruit from mainly ripe pinot noir, with a freshness and minerality that comes naturally from the soil." The result is lighter than the big, bold pinot noir styles of champagnes such as Bollinger.

"I don't feel proud of Champagne Philipponnat, I feel responsible," says Charles about the family legacy, even if the firm is now part of the same group that owns Lanson. It was acquired in 1997, three years before he joined, having been a vice president at Moët & Chandon. This begs the question – just how independent is Philipponnat? "101%!" replies Charles in a flash. "I have my own grapes, my own vineyards, my own winery, my own financing and my own distribution network."

This hands-off approach by the parent group – Lanson BCC – appears to work well, and may endure if the next generation of Philipponnats are up for the challenge.

Opposite (left): The famous champagne bottle postcard of "Les Goisses".

Opposite (right): By the early eighteenth century the Philipponnat family was supplying red wine to the court of Louis XIV.

Above: The House ages its wines in the magnificent eighteenth century cellars of the Château de Mareuil.

TASTING NOTES

RÉSERVE PERPÉTUELLE BRUT

Philipponnat rechristened its NV Brut as 'Perpétuelle' in tribute to the long tail of reserve wines that make up almost four-fifths of this pinot noir-dominated blend. Around a third spends time in oak to add some richness to the red fruit and lightly toasted character of the wine.

1522 GRAND CRU 2018

The year of 2018 had the driest of summers, with not a drop of rain from mid-June to harvest. The blend is three quarters pinot noir, and the long years bottle-ageing on the lees have added layers of brioche and pastry to this sumptuous champagne that ends with a lingering hint of spice.

PIPER-HEIDSIECK
REIMS

With its voluptuous red and gold label, Piper-Heidsieck has always sought to stand out from the crowd, and those other Heidsieck champagnes doing the rounds. Its somewhat convoluted story has been enriched by a dash of good, old-fashioned Hollywood glamour.

When Marilyn Monroe was asked what she wore in bed, her response was considered too salacious to print until 1952. Readers of *Life* magazine discovered that she slept in nothing but a drop of Chanel No. 5. "And I wake up to a glass of Piper-Heidsieck," she would sometimes add to what became a stock interview question. The image of a naked, perfumed Marilyn was so irresistible, at least to Chanel's marketing team, that the champagne reference was often glossed over.

Still, there's no doubt she loved her champagne – especially Piper-Heidsieck, then one of the biggest-selling brands in the United States. She was said to keep a month's supply in her kitchen to ensure she never ran out. The champagne was well in with the big Hollywood studios since appearing in Laurel and Hardy's *Sons of the Desert* in 1933. Piper-Heidsieck sponsored the Cannes Film Festival for almost 30 years, and the Oscars until 2021.

What began as Heidsieck & Cie was established in 1785, when there were probably fewer than 10 Champagne Houses in existence. Its founder Florenz-Ludwig (later Florens-Louis) Heidsieck dealt in fine fabrics, which he supplied to the courtiers of Versailles among others. He would travel from his home in Westphalia in Germany to Reims, one of the key textile towns in northern France, and on one of those visits, fell in love with a local girl and decided to settle there. After dabbling in champagne production for a few years, he set up his own House, and presented his wine to Queen Marie Antoinette. According to company legend it was 'love at first sip' and she became its first 'ambassador'.

When his only child died young, Florens-Louis invited his nephews to join him in business. One of them, Charles-Henri, had famously ridden on a white stallion to Moscow ahead of Napoleon's advancing army, with a stash of champagne to sell to the winning side! When old man Heidsieck died in 1828, the family firm began to fragment. In 1834 two nephews left to establish what became Heidsieck Monopole, leaving Christian Heidsieck to carry on with his partner, Henri-Guillaume Piper. Christian died a year later, and his widow then married Piper after a suitable period of mourning. Because the US market had taken to calling the brand Piper's Heidsieck, the House was officially rechristened Piper-Heidsieck in 1845.

Then, to confuse matters further, Charles-Henri's son, Charles-Camille, whose mother was from the House of Henriot, decided that he too would launch a champagne in 1851. Given that Charles Heidsieck and Piper-Heidsieck are now stablemates it makes sense to combine the two

stories. Charles Heidsieck certainly stole the limelight with his exploits in America from 1852 onwards. He was the original 'Champagne Charlie' who helped build US sales of fizz to over 300,000 bottles by the outbreak of the American Civil War, at which point his US agent stitched him up.

Charlie headed down to New Orleans to recover his debts, but got embroiled in the war and was nearly hanged as a Confederate spy. He returned home, a broken man until he suddenly received the property deeds to a third of Denver, from the brother of the US agent in an act of atonement. As Denver blossomed into a boomtown, Charlie made a fortune and his champagne business re-sparkled into life. If Champagne Charlie sounds like a movie, it is, though the 1989 rom-com starring Hugh Grant didn't do the story justice.

Yet Piper-Heidsieck became far bigger in America thanks to J. C. Kunkelmann, a long-term partner who inherited the House in 1870. Over time it passed to his granddaughter Yolande, who married the Marquis Jean de Suarez d'Aulan in 1926. As a pioneer aviator, bobsleigh champion and Resistance hero during the war, he sounds like another film script. The Marquis escaped the Gestapo by the skin of his teeth, only to be shot down in his plane above Alsace in 1945. Piper-Heidsieck was run by his son for 33 years, and since 2011 has been part of the family-owned EPI Group.

In seeking to stand-out and be different, the young *chef de caves* Émilien Boutillat has been given free rein to create a new range called Hors-Série to highlight unusual blends of old vintages and cuvées.

Opposite (top): Charles-Camille Heidsieck, or Champagne Charlie, helped popularise champagne in the United States after his made his first trip there in 1852.

Opposite (middle): Marilyn Monroe was a huge fan of the brand. It was rumoured that she kept a month's supply of Piper-Heidsieck in her kitchen, to avoid running out.

Opposite (below): A winemaker looks at champagne bottles in the Piper-Heidsieck wine cellar during the harvest in September 1945.

Above: A 1950s magazine advert with a rather orange-looking glass of fizz. Piper realised it needed bolder packaging to stand out.

TASTING NOTES

PIPER-HEIDSIECK CUVÉE BRUT

The blend of Piper's flagship champagne is half pinot noir, yet the style is somewhat fresher and lighter than that suggests. There is a breezy, crisp character to the citrus and stone fruit flavours, and maybe, if you sniff hard enough, a very feint whiff of freshly baked bread.

ESSENTIEL BLANC DE NOIRS

Four-fifths pinot noir, one-fifth pinot meunier and with a dosage of 5gms/litre, winemaker Emilien Boutillat has succeeded in creating a very precise, elegant Blanc de Noirs, with the emphasis on the red fruit flavours more than brioche, pastry notes from prolonged bottle ageing.

POL ROGER
ÉPERNAY

"Remember, gentlemen, it's not just France we are fighting for, it's champagne!" declared Winston Churchill (doubtless thinking of Pol Roger) in a famous rallying call to the troops during the Second World War. Which mattered more – the country or the drink – was unclear.

One imagines Churchill believed France was worth saving without its fizz, but perhaps not with quite the same enthusiasm. He certainly loved champagne, especially Pol Roger. If he was on two bottles a day since his first order for Pol Roger in 1908, as has been claimed, he would have drunk 42,000 bottles in his lifetime – enough to float a battleship. Add in the drip feed of diluted Johnnie Walker, dubbed 'Papa's cocktail', the early-evening Scotches, the liquid dinner, the post-prandial brandies and a highball to finish, it was a miracle he made it to middle age, let alone get Britain through its 'darkest hour'. Yet, like that other pub quiz favourite about the 250,000 cigars he allegedly smoked, the drink was at least partly a prop to demonstrate his larger-than-life capacity for booze and his cast-iron constitution.

Paul Roger, universally known as Pol, set up his wine business in the family village of Aÿ in 1849. Within three years he had moved to Épernay as Champagne Roger, which he ran until his two sons took over in 1899. Georges and Maurice, who changed the family name to Pol-Roger, inherited a thriving business with a royal warrant from Queen Victoria granted in 1877. Pol Roger was served in the grand hotels along the Champs-Élysées and in London's West End, and in the House of Commons, where Winston Churchill possibly discovered it.

As mayor of Épernay, Maurice Pol-Roger had to cope with the Germans when they marched into town on 4 September 1914. He was held hostage and threatened with execution four times before the Germans left a week later, having been defeated in the Battle of the Marne. Pol-Roger and his friends at Perrier-Jouët immediately set about organising the harvest as artillery shells whizzed and roared in the background. And so it was throughout the war, with grapes picked every vintage. While Épernay escaped the devastation suffered by Reims, a hundred bombs fell one summer's day in 1917, and the entire population took refuge in the cellars of Pol Roger and Perrier-Jouët.

The Churchill connection was cemented in the next war at a party in Paris after the city's liberation in August 1944. The wartime leader was completely captivated by Odette Pol-Roger. She was a renowned society beauty and Maurice's daughter-in-law. Were they more than just friends? "Well, I'm sure he fancied her," says James Simpson, head of Pol Roger (UK). "But no, it was 'a harmless, late autumn friendship' as someone called it." Churchill promised to stamp the grapes with his own bare feet if he were ever invited to what he called "the world's most drinkable address". Sadly he never made it to Épernay, but Odette made sure he was supplied with a case every birthday of his favourite vintage – 1928 – until it ran out. In return he named his favourite racehorse Pol Roger in her honour.

The Champagne House responded in kind by releasing its Sir Winston Churchill vintage cuvée for the first time in 1975, 10 years after his death. A black border appeared on the label and remained there for years. The House came out of mourning only in 2003, when it won back the royal warrant that had lapsed in the 1930s. "Yet even now, we get some old codger complaining about us removing the armband," says Simpson.

The House is still in family hands, thanks in no small part to owning 91 hectares of vineyards, or half its needs for its 2 million bottle production. Simpson concedes there may be a slight over-reliance on one famous customer, but says:

> *"If all people ever remember about Pol Roger is that it's family-owned and Churchill drank it, that's a whole lot more than most other champagnes."*

It is certainly a very traditional House which still believes in riddling its bottles and labelling its Cuvée Sir Winston Churchill by hand. Apparently there are just six full-time riddlers living in Épernay, four of them employed by Pol Roger.

Opposite: A case of Winston Churchill's favourite champagne, Pol Roger, being delivered to his Hyde Park home on his 87th birthday.

Above (left): As a medium-sized Champagne House, with an annual production of 1.6 million bottles, Pol Roger's 91 hectares of vineyards are enough to satisfy half of its needs.

Above (right): The House's sumptuous head office in Épernay, at 44 Avenue Champagne, which, according to Churchill, was "the most drinkable address in the world".

TASTING NOTES

POL ROGER BRUT RÉSERVE NV

Pol Roger bills this wine as "‘the perfect apéritif champagne", and it certainly has the fresh, youthful vigour to sharpen the taste buds. The elegance is supplied by the third that is Côte des Blancs chardonnay, while an equal measure of Montage de Reims pinot noir adds to the crunchy red apple fruit.

POL ROGER BRUT VINTAGE 2018

In Pol Roger's traditional style, this is grand and premier cru pinot noir from the Montagne de Reims with 40% chardonnay from the Côte des Blancs, aged in its deepest cellars. The initial fresh fruits on the nose give way to layers of brioche and citrus notes on the tongue.

POMMERY
REIMS

Louise Pommery was a force of nature not unlike the mighty Veuve Clicquot. You might not guess from her widow's weeds and stern expression in her portraits, but she proved to be one of the most flamboyant brand-builders in the history of champagne.

Veuve Clicquot was a big brand by the mid-nineteenth century with sales of more than 400,000 bottles a year, and its namesake, the widow Barbe Nicole, still very much involved in her seventies. Soon a new champagne widow was on the scene, every bit as determined as Veuve Clicquot herself.

The story starts with a small Champagne House called Dubois-Gosset, which Narcisse Greno took over in 1836. While Greno took care of sales and marketing, the financial backing came from Louis Alexandre Pommery, scion of a wealthy textile family in Reims. Pommery came to own the majority, and when he died in 1858, his widow Louise assumed control.

Veuve Pommery was approaching 40, while the firm of Pommery & Greno was more into wool than wine, the latter more still than sparkling. Louise soon changed that as she and her faithful assistant, Henri Vasnier, propelled Champagne Pommery into the big time. It became particularly popular in the UK, where it helped pioneer the taste for brut champagne.

Her physical legacy is the company's colossal, castle-like HQ on tunnels carved out of the *crayères*, or chalk and limestone quarries dug by the Romans, which she bought from the Ruinarts. Claude Ruinart had simply stored his wine there, but Madame Pommery decided to turn them into a 'Theatre of Champagne' that became one of the top tourist attractions in France. The scale and industrial self-confidence of the enterprise recalls Victorian shipyards on the Clyde, though it has to be said champagne has endured rather better.

Visitors gasped at the collection of turrets and spires – an architectural pick 'n' mix of Scots Baronial and Disneyland – before descending a grand staircase into the cellar. There are bas-reliefs carved into the walls and vast wooden blending vats. Bottles stretch off into the gloom along boulevards named after some of the key cities Pommery supplied: Dublin, Buenos Aires and Havana.

Meanwhile, above ground, Madame Pommery had begun to accumulate vineyards and to wean the British on to *brut*-style champagne. "Damas, we need a wine that is as dry as possible, but without rigidity," she wrote to her *chef de cave*, Olivier Damas. "It should be soft and velvety on the palate ... Above all, make sure it has finesse." The wine, created by his successor, Victor Lambert, was the 1874 Pommery Nature that was sold in England two years later.

Whether Pommery 'invented' brut or not, this particular bottle certainly did more than any to shift English tastes that way. In France, Germany and above all Russia, champagne long remained something sweet and fizzy for the end of the meal. In England, 20 years after the release of Pommery '74, *Vanity Fair* was lamenting that: "never more such wine may pass our lips". Madame Pommery died in 1890, having married her daughter Louise to Prince Guy de Polignac, who was as blue-blooded as they come and cousin to Monaco's ruling family, the Grimaldis.

With global sales of more than two million bottles and pole position in the UK, Pommery was in fine shape for the next generation that included Louis Pommery, his sister Louise and her well-connected husband. Between them they expanded the vineyards to 300 hectares, second only to the holding of Moët & Chandon.

By 1907 the next generation – Melchior de Polignac – was in charge and it remained in his descendants' hands until 1979, when the fertiliser tycoon Xavier Gardinier bought Pommery and Lanson. All members of the family were culled from the business apart from Alain de Polignac, who remained as winemaker, and who later created the luxury Cuvée Louise in honour of the famous widow.

Owning both Lanson and Pommery proved too much for the Gardiniers, and in 1984, they sold their stake to the French multinational BSN, which, six years later, passed both brands on to LVMH. Pommery was subsequently acquired by Paul-François Vranken in 2002, and is now stablemates with Heidsieck-Monopole and Vranken Champagne. Under Vranken's leadership the historic vineyards of Madame Pommery have been preserved, while her somewhat neglected husband lives on as Louis Pommery Brut. Crafted by cellarmaster, Clément Pierlot, it was the first English sparkler ever to be released by a Champagne House in 2020.

Opposite (left): The sprawling headquarters of Champagne Pommery on the eastern outskirts of Reims, resembles Walt Disney's Magic Kingdom.

Opposite (right): The redoubtable Madame Louise Pommery, who inherited the House in 1858, and went on to become one of the great champagne widows in the mould of Veuve Clicquot.

Right: Rare bottles of vintage Pommery in the House's cellar. Today Pommery produces somewhere in the region of five million bottles of champagne per annum.

TASTING NOTES

POMMERY BRUT ROYAL NV

The boldly packaged Brut Royal is an equal blend of the three champagne grapes given three years ageing on its lees. The result is a classic apéritif style that is delicate, ethereal and gently floral on the nose with a taut, lively core of crunchy red fruit.

POMMERY APANAGE 1874

This new cuvée was launched in 2024 as a blend of Pommery's reserve wine and three vintages back to 2012. It comes from cru villages of mainly chardonnay and pinot noir and offers a toasty, floral aroma with a fine, silky mousse and long, zesty finish. Created as a 'gourmet champagne', it's not a bad aperitif either.

LOUIS ROEDERER
REIMS

Little is known about Dubois Père & Fils whose tiny Champagne House, founded in 1760, was inherited by Louis Roederer in 1833. Under its new guise it became one of the most revered names in champagne thanks partly to its superlative prestige cuvée, Cristal.

Unlike most of his fellow merchants, Roederer believed in acquiring vineyards at a time when grape prices were so low it seemed to make little economic sense to do so. "I think he had this vision of making the best champagne possible, and the way to do that was to own your own vineyards in the best Grand Cru sites," believes Frédéric Rouzard, the current boss and now the seventh generation in charge. Of his ancestor's first purchase – 15 hectares in Verzenay – he says: "Today they're recognised as one of the best sites for pinot noir in Champagne."

Rouzard has added another 25 hectares to bring Roederer's current total to around 240 hectares. They stretch from the south-facing slopes of the Marne valley in Mareuil, Aÿ and other villages, to top chardonnay sites in the Côte des Blancs, and the pinot noir heartlands of the Montagne de Reims. With a production of around 3 million bottles a year, the firm's own grapes supply 70% of its requirements, and all its needs in the case of its vintage wines. More than two-thirds of the vineyards are Grand Cru.

When his great-grandmother, Camille Olry-Roederer, was on the prowl for new vineyards in the 1930s there were growers desperate to sell. Today it has become a great deal harder, as Rouzard concedes. With grapes now selling for more than €7 a kilo, the asking price for even a couple of rows of Grand Cru vines has reached eye-popping levels. Rivals with fewer vineyards might suggest the secret to great champagne lies more in the cellar where the cuvées are constructed, than in the land – yet behind the scenes one suspects they covet Roederer's magnificent estate.

By the second half of the nineteenth century, champagne's biggest foreign customers after the British were the Russians. It was a market first developed by Veuve Clicquot and her salesman Louis Bohn, but despite their best efforts other champagnes seeped in, including Louis Roederer. In the 1870s the House was asked to create an exclusive cuvée for the Russian emperor, Alexander II. The best and oldest vineyards were selected, but all their goodness was buried beneath a ton of sugar by the time Cristal was presented to the Czar in 1876. The Russians liked their champagnes sweeter than Coke, which contains 106g/litre of sugar.

Cristal was named after the clear Baccarat crystal, chosen to make the bottle stand out when wrapped in linen at imperial banquets. There was also no punt – the deep indentation at the bottom of a bottle – lest anyone attempt to conceal a grenade. The Czar's paranoia was justified: he was assassinated in 1881 after numerous attempts. Roederer remained the official champagne of the imperial court, and Russian sales accounted for a third of production until the Revolution in 1917. It seems there were hefty unpaid bills, which strangely enough the Bolsheviks never settled.

Cristal, no longer in Baccarat crystal because it proved too weak but still with its flat bottom, was relaunched in 1924. With America lost to Prohibition and then the Depression, Louis Roederer was almost bankrupt by the early 1930s, when Camille Olry-Roederer inherited from her late husband. The House was haemorrhaging money thanks to her brother-in-law, who was living like the Sun King as though the Russian Revolution had never happened. So she sacked him. "Imagine the scandal!" says Rouzard. "A woman! Who in those days didn't even have the vote."

The story of Cristal moved on from Russian Czars to rap stars and an unfortunate spat with Jay-Z. The rapper took offence at a comment by Rouzard in 2006, and began dissing his once favourite champagne in favour of gold-plated bottles of Armand de Brignac Ace of Spades, which he now happens to own. Demand for Cristal was undented, unlike during the financial crash that followed.

Today the wine comes from almost entirely biodynamic vineyards and is given a modest dosage of 9g/litre to allow Roederer to fulfil its simple pledge: "to extract the magic of the Grand Cru", in Rouzard's words. Roederer has been promoting biodiversity in its vineyards for almost 30 years. In the coming decades everything will gradually be replanted with vines from its own nursery to help give the vineyards the natural resilience to cope with climate change. Meanwhile the House has released a pair of wines called Camille in tribute to its very own champagne widow, and a new, top-of-the-range Cristal Vinothèque.

Opposite (left): Through the careful accumulation of vineyards, Roederer now owns 240 hectares of Champagne, which accounts for around two-thirds of its needs.

Opposite (right): Rare bottles of vintage Pommery in the House's cellar. Today Pommery produces somewhere in the region of five million bottles of champagne per annum.

Right: Louis Roederer Cristal – the world's first prestige *cuvée* – created for Czar Alexander II in the 1870s as an exclusive champagne for the Imperial Russian court. It was later relaunched to a wider audience in 1924.

TASTING NOTES

LOUIS ROEDERER COLLECTION 245 NV

Wine from 2020 – the 245th year since Roederer was founded – was blended with the *'réserve perpetuelle'*, a solera-like tank of older vintages to give a ripeness and maturity to this mix of chardonnay and pinot noir with an aroma of apples and citrus peel.

LOUIS ROEDERER VINTAGE BRUT 2016

All from Roederer's own vineyards – led by pinot noir, especially from Verzy in the Montagne de Reims, and supported by chardonnay from the Côte des Blancs cru of Chouilly – this is a fine-textured, complex wine of red fruits, nuts and brioche with a mineral, slightly salty edge.

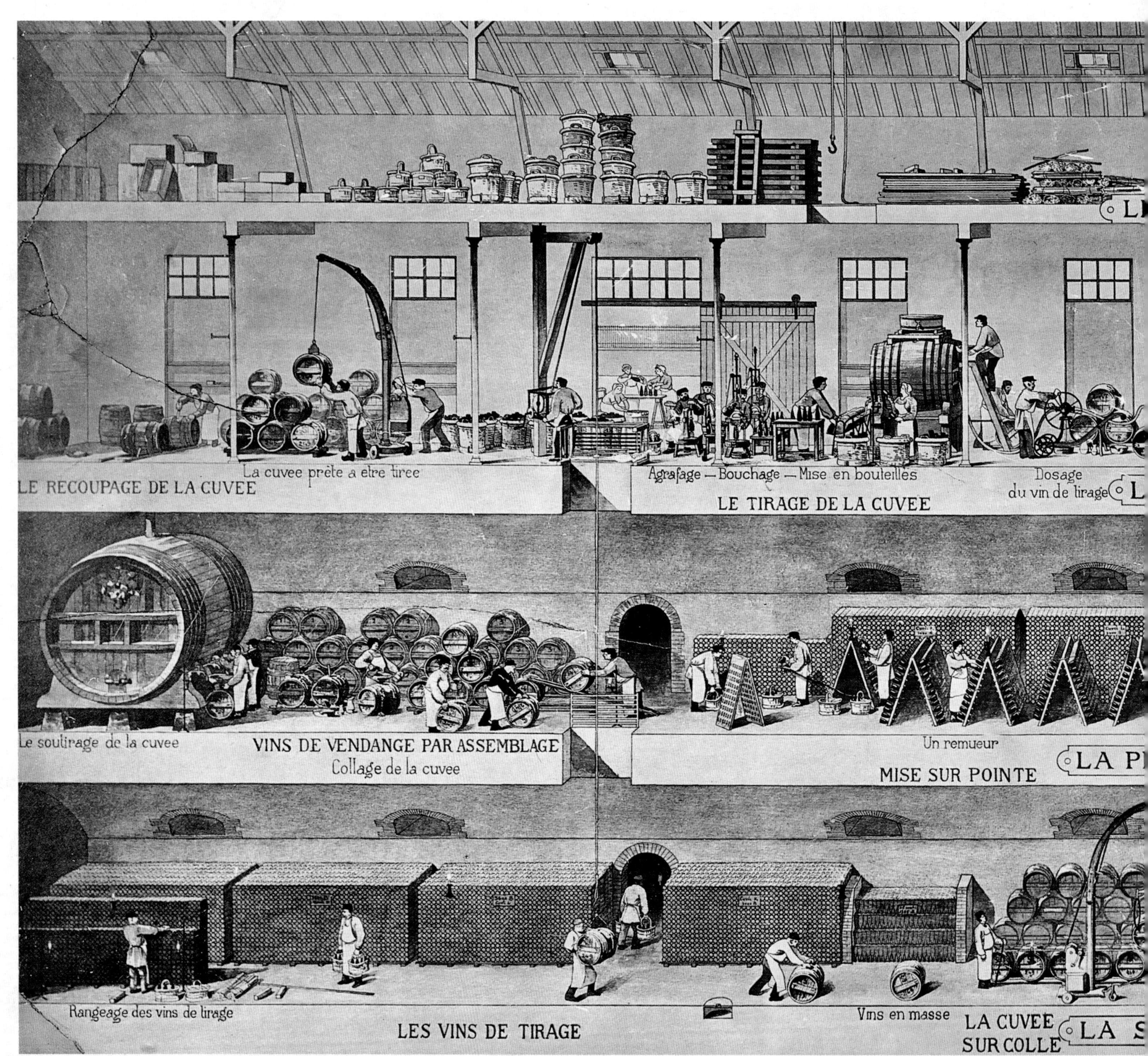

Above: Everything under one roof at Roederer – from the bags of corks under the eaves to the vats of reserve wine deep in the cellar.

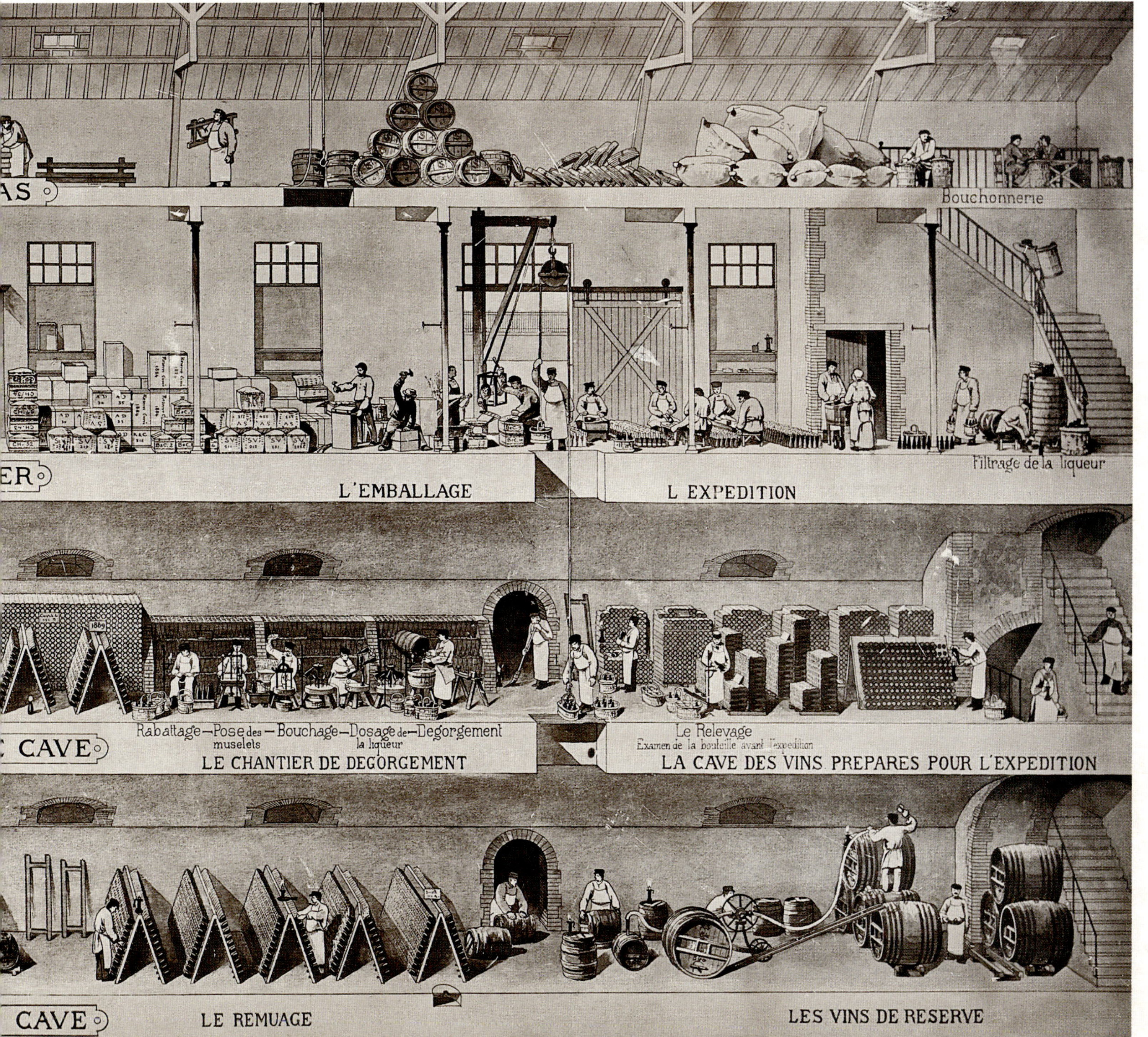

Bouchonnerie
L'EMBALLAGE
L EXPEDITION
Filtrage de la liqueur
CAVE
Rabattage—Pose des muselets—Bouchage—Dosage de la liqueur—Degorgement
LE CHANTIER DE DEGORGEMENT
Le Relevage
Examen de la bouteille avant l'expedition
LA CAVE DES VINS PREPARES POUR L'EXPEDITION
CAVE
LE REMUAGE
LES VINS DE RESERVE

RUINART
REIMS

Maison Ruinart is the oldest active Champagne House. It remained in family hands for over two centuries until bought out by Moët & Chandon in 1963. Perhaps better known in France than elsewhere, it is a well-respected House famed for the seamless purity of its Ruinart Blanc des Blancs.

In the early eighteenth century sparkling champagne was restricted by the ban on transporting wine in bottles. Of course, this did not stop the English adding some sugar to the casks they imported to provoke a secondary fermentation and a few bubbles. But as far as the French are concerned, the story begins in 1728, when the ban on bottled wine was lifted by royal decree.

Nicolas Ruinart, a draper from Reims, wasted no time in setting up the first Champagne House in 1729. Initially just a sideline – he used to give bottles away as gifts to his textile clients – within six years it became his main business, and by 1760 he was selling 36,000 bottles a year. The inspiration had been his uncle, Dom Ruinart, a Benedictine monk who had studied at the Abbey of Saint-Germain-des-Prés near Paris. Apparently, having observed the Parisian courtiers enjoying this new vice, he convinced his nephew that there was money to be had from "wine with bubbles".

His fellow Champenois took almost a century to be convinced and even then a few diehards refused to sparkle. Yet from champagne's magnificent debut in art, in Jean-François de Troy's *Le Déjeuner d'huîtres* (The Oyster Lunch, see page 31), it's clear there were some early adopters. The bottle on the table was undeniably sparkling – in fact, a true *saut-bouchon* (cork-jumper) if you study the painting carefully.

Frédéric Panaiotis, the current *chef de cave*, would like to think they were drinking Ruinart, being one of only two Houses in existence by the time of the painting in 1735. If the other – Chanoine – has evidence to the contrary he would love to hear from them. Ruinart was the first to invest in Gallo-Roman chalk cellars, and now has 8km of tunnels beneath Reims. It was also the pioneer of rosé champagne way back in 1764. Yet Panaiotis is keen not to be trapped by the past.

"Being the oldest means we have to keep being modern," he says. "I think the style of our wine is pretty modern. It's very pure, very fruit-driven and with a lot of chardonnay." As a jazz-lover he sees something of that cool American saxophonist, Stan Getz, in Ruinart. Maybe try a glass while listening to 'The Girl from Ipanema', and you'll see it too.

There has also been a long connection with modern art since André Ruinart commissioned the Czech artist Alphonse Mucha in 1896 to paint a series of posters featuring a beautiful, near-life-size woman with wild, coiling locks of hair holding a champagne coupe amidst a profusion of bubbles. Today the House sponsors contemporary art fairs, and displays over 100 works of art in the buildings and grounds of its new Nicolas

Ruinart Pavilion. The landscaped gardens are open to all.

In 1919 André Ruinart died, leaving his young English wife, Mary Kate Charlotte Riboldi, Viscountess Ruinart de Brimont, to try and rebuild the House after the devastation of war. She was from a humble background, and had been orphaned at an early age. Aside from the almost complete flattening of Reims under the German artillery, Ruinart had lost one important market after the Russian Revolution, and was about to lose another a year later. The US Congress had just ratified the Volstead Act, which led to Prohibition in January 1920.

For the next five years Viscountess Charlotte helped keep Ruinart afloat until her son was old enough to take over. Today Ruinart has access to some wonderful grapes, especially Grand Cru chardonnay from the Montagne de Reims.

Chardonnay is clearly the signature grape of Ruinart, which offers a range of Blanc de Blancs including the new Blanc Singulier, "which is made in the hottest years to show the effects of climate change," explains Panaiotis. "Even though it's zero dosage, it's actually very friendly to drink." Behind the scenes, as throughout the region, he and his team are experimenting with clonal selection and different vine training systems to prolong the positive impact of global warming. Ruinart will be doing all it can to preserve its house style of 'aromatic freshness'.

Panaiotis insists Ruinart has a clear identity. "We're the house of chardonnay," he says, describing the House style as one of "aromatic freshness". It certainly deserves to be better known.

Opposite: The Ruinart champagne celler.

Top: The entrance to Ruinart in Reims.

Left: The first established Champagne House was founded by Nicolas Ruinart, a draper from Reims, in 1729.

TASTING NOTES

RUINART BLANC DE BLANCS NV

The House likes to claim that chardonnay is "the very soul of Ruinart", and this is certainly one of the top NV Blanc de Blancs with its racy acidity and peach and pear flavours. There's an almost fleshy character, perhaps from the Montagne de Reim's grapes, and a trace of chalk and wet stones.

DOM RUINART BLANC DE BLANCS 2013

After a cool spring and early summer, the grapes were finally picked at the end September. The result is a youthful, vigorous wine brimming with freshness and *joie de vivre*. It is almost mouth-watering on the tongue with its burst of citrus fruit and lemon zest, slowly fading to a dry, mineral finish.

Caves
Ruinart Père & Fils
Reims
Les Plus
Pittoresques
de la Champagne
Visite Libre
Imp. F. Champenois, Paris.

Opposite: Painted by Louis Tauzin in 1914, just before the First World War, the poster proclaims Ruinart's cellars to be "the most picturesque in Champagne".

Left: The Czech painter Alphonse Mucha's famous Art Deco poster for the brand (c.1898).

TAITTINGER
REIMS

From an almost standing start in the dark days of the 1930s, Taittinger has risen to become the sixth-largest Champagne House with annual sales pushing six million bottles. Within the corporate world of champagne, its approach is as refreshing as its sensual, chardonnay-based wines.

“Sex has played a huge role in the success of champagne. You can trace it back to the mistresses of Louis XIV,” the former president of Champagne Taittinger once told *Decanter* magazine.

Pierre-Emmanuel Taittinger was clearly a breath of fresh air amidst the corporate suits of Champagne – a man full of passion, warmth and wit who joined the family firm in 1976. The House was founded 44 years earlier by his grandfather Pierre Taittinger, who had been billeted at the Château de la Marquetterie near Épernay as a young officer during the First World War.

After the war he managed to buy the Château and its few hectares of vineyards, followed by the acquisition of the champagne Forest & Fourneaux, founded in 1734, which he eventually rechristened Taittinger. The family also bought and restored the home of the Counts of Champagne in Reims, and moved in in 1933. And it acquired the thirteenth-century cellars of the St Niçaise Abbey, where its Comtes de Champagne cuvée is aged.

Before and after the Second World War, Pierre and his sons, Jean and François, embarked on a great vineyard buying spree. “It was very much a strategic decision,” says Pierre-Emmanuel’s son, Clovis Taittinger, now joint-MD alongside his sister Vitalie, now president. It was evidently a good time to buy land when prices were nothing compared to the €1.5 million or so charged for a hectare of decent vineyards today, and Taittinger now has 288 of them. Around 70 are in the Aube, where they began acquiring good-quality sites for chardonnay and pinot noir in the 1960s, long before most of their rivals.

By this stage Claude Taittinger was in charge. “It was Claude who developed the revolutionary style that was fresh and elegant,” says Clovis. “At the time champagne was very much pinot-driven and used old-style *barriques*, while Taittinger was sophisticated, feminine and chardonnay-based. It was without wood, without make-up and very sexy.” His father once caused a frisson in the land of the draconian, anti-alcohol *Loi Évin*, by claiming that champagne’s stiffest competition came not from other sparkling wines but from Viagra.

The pinnacle of Taittinger’s faith in chardonnay is found in its Comtes de Champagne Blanc de Blancs, a vintage blend from five Grand Cru villages including Avize, Cramant and Le Mesnil-sur-Oger which was first released in 1952. A soupçon of spice and creamy texture is added from 5%

of the wine being matured in new oak, and the whole is aged for 10 years in the cellar. A Comtes de Champagne rosé was added in 1966, and this contains 70% pinot noir from prime sites in the Montaigne de Reims.

The extended family had been growing the group to include prestigious hotels, like the Crillon in Paris, a Perfume House and Baccarat Crystal. With this added financial muscle and its base of vineyards, Taittinger's position seemed to be rock-solid when Pierre-Emanuel took over from his uncle Claude in 1998. But cracks were opening up beneath the surface and, when an American hotel chain bid for the group in 2005, six of the seven branches of the family voted "yes". But the Americans didn't want the champagne, and soon it was back on the market. With help from the local Crédit Agricole, Pierre-Emmanuel somehow beat off 10 global bids and managed to buy back Taittinger for €660 million in May 2006. To celebrate he claims to have shared a bottle of Comtes de Champagne with his wife and daughter, and danced round the dining-room table in his underpants.

Clovis denies the last part, perhaps blocking out memories of an embarrassing dad, but either way the news went down well in Champagne. Nine years later Taittinger made history by becoming the first House to plant an English vineyard – Domaine Evremond in Kent, in a joint-venture with its UK importer, Hatch Mansfield.

Opposite (above): The neat, corrugated slopes of the 250 hectares belonging to Taittinger.

Opposite (below): The House's thirteenth-century wine cellars beneath the St Niçaise Abbey are now a Unesco World Heritage site; it is here that the famous *Comtes de Champagne* cuvée has been aged since the 1960s.

Above (left): The Château de la Marquetterie, near Épernay, so called for its patchwork vineyards of black and white grapes.

Above (left): Grace Kelly shows off her curves for Comtes de Champagne – Taittinger's top-of-the-range Blanc de Blancs launched in 1952.

TASTING NOTES

TAITTINGER PRESTIGE ROSÉ NV

This relatively new blend of Taittinger Rose involves a gentle maceration of pinot noir from Ambonnay, Verzennay, Hautvillers and Les Riceys, with chardonnay and pinot meunier. There are supple tannins, and redcurrant flavours, as suggested by the colour, but also peach and citrus too.

TAITTINGER COMTES DE CHAMPAGNE BLANC DE BLANCS 2013

It's hard not to be swept away by the sheer veuve and elegance of this vintage of Taittinger's most prestigious cuvee. From its floral, spring-like charm on the nose, to its refreshing bite of acidity that softens with brioche and apple pie notes, it is intensely moreish and not a little delicious.

VEUVE CLICQUOT
REIMS

In the space of a generation the widowed Madame Clicquot took a small Champagne House in Reims in 1805 and propelled it to stardom. Now part of the luxury brand empire LVMH, Veuve Clicquot continues to live up to her legacy 150 years after her death.

Widowed at 27 with a three-year-old daughter and a business to run, Barbe Nicole Clicquot Ponsardin's story reads like a film script – a plucky single mum who, in a man's world and against all odds, builds one of the most powerful champagne brands of all time. Back at the dawn of the nineteenth century when the tale begins, however, the key point was not 'single mum' but 'widow', as the makers of the Netflix biopic *Widow Cliquot* realised.

The House was founded in 1772 by Philippe Clicquot, whose son François-Marie built up sales to 60,000 bottles by 1804. A comfortable life beckoned for Barbe Nicole, his well-connected wife whose father was a wealthy textile merchant and mayor of Reims. But François-Marie died a year later, leaving his widowed bride the chance to shine as one of the great champagne entrepreneurs. With Europe at war and the English navy blockading the seas, trade links to exciting new markets among the Baltic States and beyond were cut off. Things looked bleak, and as her devoted salesman, Louis Bohn, wrote: "Business is terribly stagnant ... prices are plummeting."

Then, streaking high above the vineyards, came the Great Comet of 1811, which Barbe Nicole took as an omen for an exceptional vintage. She was determined that her wine's newfound Russian admirers should not be denied despite the Czar's boycott of French wines in 1812. A Dutch ship was chartered with instructions to carry no other champagne but 10,550 bottles of Veuve Clicquot to the Baltic port of Königsberg. Without waiting to hear news, the canny widow dispatched another 12,000 a week later.

You are "the terror of all your competitors", wrote an ecstatic Louis Bohn as he described the Russians "with their tongues hanging out" to taste the Comet vintage. Soon he was boasting of Veuve Clicquot's spring-like clarity thanks to *chef de cave* Antoine-Aloys Müller, who had perfected the technique of *remuage* (the removal of the yeasty sediment) by riddling the bottles in a specially made *pupitre*. Whether or not he actually drilled holes in Barbe Nicole's desk to make the device, she was thrilled and tried hard to keep it a secret.

She failed in that but did succeed, unlike Napoleon, in conquering Russia, which became champagne's second-biggest export market after Britain, and helped propel Veuve Clicquot's sales to more than 400,000 bottles by 1850. That year, sensing that her daughter and son-in-law, the Comte de Chevigné, wouldn't be able to cope, she handed the business to her partner, Edouard Werlé. The Comte had discovered a wonderful way of extracting money from his wealthy mother-in-law to pay off his gambling debts.

Veuve Clicquot died in 1866, but the brand lived on under Werlé and his descendants. Sales had topped three million bottles by 1900 thanks to Russia and its growing success in the United States. That number has since soared to an estimated 18 million bottles, of which around 15 million is the famous egg-yolk 'Yellow Label' trademarked in 1877. The colour is defended with litigious zeal lest anyone come close to Pantone 137C. An exception is made for Glenmorangie Single Malt, for that too is owned by LVMH following its acquisition of Veuve Clicquot in 1986.

A year later, Veuve Clicquot released its first prestige cuvée – La Grande Dame, in tribute to the widow herself. Two-thirds pinot noir, it comes from eight special Grand Cru sites in Aÿ, Verzenay, Ambonnay and Bouzy, from within the House's 393 hectares that supply one-fifth of its needs.

The 'Yellow Label' has become drier with a *dosage* down from 12g to 9g/litre, a fraction of the sugary 150g Veuve Clicquot once guzzled by the Romanovs. Yet bridging the gap is Veuve Clicquot Rich with its 60g/litre of sugar in a glitzy silver bottle. Its sweetness is designed for drinking over ice and with one added garnish, for a younger generation, perhaps weaned on prosecco. True to its roots, Veuve Cliquot has a proud history of supporting female entrepreneurs with its Bold Woman awards, while recent partnerships have included Stella McCartney creating bags from a grape-based alternative leather sourced from the vineyards.

Opposite (left): Veuve Clicquot's palatial headquarters in Reims, a testament to the ruthless determination of its namesake and the success of her brand in nineteenth-century Russia.

Opposite (right): This staircase, descending to Clicquot's cellars, is marked with all of the Champagne House's declared vintage years.

Left: A magazine advertisement from the 1930s, promoting the distinctly orange 'Yellow Label' of the flagship brand, whose sales are now estimated at around 15 million bottles a year.

TASTING NOTES

VEUVE CLICQUOT BRUT NV

The world-famous 'Yellow Label' and centrepiece of the Veuve Clicquot collection has instantly recognisable flavour, power and consistency. It is a reliable crowd-pleaser with its supple texture and red-apple crunch of acidity, which gains complexity if you lay it down for a few years.

VEUVE CLICQUOT LA GRANDE DAME 2015

This long-established tribute to the widow is now almost a Blanc de Noirs with just 10% chardonnay to provide sufficient bite and acidity for long-ageing. There are flinty, mineral aromas along with green apples that turn more citrus on the tongue, along with some honey and sweet spice.

BEHIND THE BUBBLES

Of course, the champagne trade is infinitely larger and more complex than the previous pages might suggest. There are other more famous brands, or Grandes Marques, to consider, alongside a number of popular champagnes, like Jacquart and Nicolas Feuillatte, produced by the cooperatives, and a vast sea of smaller, grower champagnes.

To help navigate our way through champagne, it is worth considering the structure of the trade and how it has evolved. Today there are just over 16,000 growers who own 90% of the 34,000 hectares of vineyards within the *appellation*. None of the major champagne Houses is self-sufficient in grapes, and while some like Roederer and Bollinger own two-thirds of their needs, some have no vineyards at all. The Houses, of which there are around 300, own just over 3,100 hectares between them, yet they sell two-thirds of all champagne and 90% of exports.

In 1882 the Syndicat du Commerce des Vins de Champagne was established to defend the wine and its geographic roots. The name 'champagne' risked becoming as generic as eau de Cologne with producers outside the region happily using the c-word. Membership of the Syndicat was theoretically open to any négociant, or champagne merchant in the Marne, and basically included anyone of any standing in the trade. Eventually, in 1964, an elite emerged, calling itself the Syndicat des Grandes Marques de Champagne. Among the original 25 grandees on the list were Bollinger, Krug, Perrier-Jouët and Louis Roederer. Another five, including Canard-Duchêne and Gosset, were added later. As with the Royal Enclosure during Royal Ascot's horse race meeting, admission was strictly by invitation only.

This self-appointed champagne aristocracy was officially disbanded in 1997, because its members were unable to agree the precise quality criteria on which they could base their alleged superiority. However, the term 'Grande Marque' lives on as a reference to the big, traditional brands. The relationship between the growers in Champagne and the champagne Houses who control the market, particularly abroad, has

always been complicated. On their own, individual growers, with less than two hectares of vines between them on average, appear powerless compared to the big brand-owners. But collectively, the growers clearly have strength in numbers, and this is what inspired them to form cooperatives to obtain the greatest value for their key asset – the grapes.

The number of cooperatives has swollen to over 130 of which just over a third sell their own wine with annual sales pushing 30 million bottles. They represent 16,000 growers who tend approximately 45% of Champagne's vineyards. The co-ops play a key role as middlemen between the growers and the négociants or Houses, allowing them to sign big contracts for grapes or *vin clair* (base wine) rather than the never-ending hassle of signing thousands of them with the individual growers. The advantage for the grower is that his or her cooperative can use its muscle to obtain the best price for the grapes. At present grapes fetch upwards of €7 per kilo, of which you need 1.2kg per 75cl bottle, or 1.5kg if you are using just the first pressing of grapes.

The strongest cooperatives have developed their own brands in direct competition to the established names, and recognisable by a 'CM' on the label. Nicolas Feuillatte, owned by the region's biggest cooperative with 5,000 members, is now the world's top-selling champagne behind Moët and Veuve Clicquot. If it grows much bigger, you wonder if some of those who rely on the cooperative for fruit may go thirsty. Meanwhile, among the thousands of growers, few have not at some stage dreamed of making their own champagne, rather than simply selling their produce for others to bottle. In lean times, with plummeting demand for their fruit, it was not so much a dream as a dire necessity to make wine. The growers had to do something with their leftover grapes. In good times, with grape prices far higher than in other wine regions, that incentive has clearly reduced.

Then again, if others are surfing a great surge in demand for champagne and reaping the rewards, why not join in if you have sufficient vineyards in the right place and the confidence to give it a try? The up-front costs in equipment and having to tie up money in stock are obvious barriers to entry, and while making wine is relatively straightforward, selling it is anything but. Grower champagnes' share has been slowly shrinking since 2000 when it accounted for 26% of the market. Most of the sales are in France where champagne consumption has contracted sharply in recent years, and many are daunted by the immense cost and effort involved in exports. And yet a few dozen have broken through, and as craft brewers and boutique distillers have proved, there's certainly some antipathy towards big brands these days. With their terroir-driven approach, some grower champagnes have achieved cult status among top sommeliers and on the blogosphere.

Opposite: The balance of power in Champagne lies between the big brands who dominate the market, particularly abroad, and the growers who own 90% of the vineyards. Today more than 2,000 growers produce their own wine under their own label.

Above: Within 40 years of its launch, Nicolas Feuillate has become a massive, 10-million-bottle brand. Owned by the region's biggest cooperative, it poses a direct challenge to the long-established grandees of Champagne.

OTHER FAMOUS CHAMPAGNE HOUSES

There are plenty more Champagne Houses to consider, ranging from the boutique end of the spectrum to big names that have suffered in the consolidation among the key brand owners. Some have emerged, stripped of their vineyards, yet determined to reclaim their reputation under new ownership.

While other champagnes competed to supply the courts and principalities of Europe, **Mercier** was aimed at the burgeoning middle classes, particularly in France. Eugène Mercier grouped together five small Champagne Houses in 1858, and then created his own brand. He built a large, functional winery with direct access to the railways in 1871, and two decades later took the Paris Exhibition by storm with his most famous publicity stunt. This was the 'world's biggest blending vat' that took seven years to build and was towed from Épernay to Paris by 24 white oxen. Ever since then it has been one of the biggest-selling champagnes in France, a market that accounts for around 80% of its sales. The House accumulated 220 hectares of vineyards, with the most planted variety being pinot meunier. This is said to explain the soft, youthful, easy-drinking style of Mercier Brut NV. In 1970 Moët & Chandon bought the brand, and to some extent treated it as a *sous marque*, or second label, even though it still comfortably outsells Moët in the domestic market.

Eight years after Mercier was swallowed up by what is now LVMH, Veuve Clicquot did the same to **Canard-Duchêne**. The House was founded in the village of Ludes on the northern flank of the Montagne de Reims in 1868 after the marriage of a cooper called Victor Canard and Léonie Duchêne, whose family were growers. The grand crest on the label came from the Imperial Russian Court once supplied by the House. A century later it was on semi-permanent special offer in French supermarkets where many of the two million-plus bottles were sold. Today it is the second biggest-selling champagne brand in France.

In 2003 the House was bought, and some might say rescued, by Alain Thiénot, a former champagne broker, who had been quietly building up

Below (left): Mercier currently owns 220 hectares of vineyards within its LVMH stable, the most planted grape variety being pinot meunier.

Below: Eugène Mercier, who founded Mercier in 1858, aged just 20, built it into one of the most powerful champagne brands of all.

his own champagne empire since 1981. With Canard-Duchêne he became a much bigger player, but his new purchase was clearly in need of some TLC. Cellar master Laurent Fédou has freshened up the House style, while the large, somewhat industrial-looking cellars in Ludes have been much improved. Meanwhile the group has been building its own brand: Champagne Thiénot, launched in 1985 and also made by Fédou.

Another large House, is that of **G.H. Martel**, now based in Reims and founded a year after Canard-Duchêne in 1869. It was really developed by André Tabourin from the 1920s until his death in 1979, when the firm was sold to the Rapeneau family who went on to acquire Charles de Cazenove champagne in 2003. Today Martel owns some 200 hectares of vineyards planted with mainly chardonnay and pinot noir, which supplies around one-fifth of its needs. The brand is much better known in France than in the UK or the United States, and is often on offer in the supermarkets. In 1989 it decided to launch a well-regarded good value prestige cuvée called Cuvée Victoire.

Up in the Montagne de Reims in the village of Chigny-les-Roses – as floral as it sounds – the **Cattier** family have been growers since the eighteenth century, finally becoming producers after the First World War. Today they own around 35 hectares, mainly in premier cru vineyards in Chigny-les-Roses, Rilly-la-Montagne, Taissy and Ludes, with half given over to pinot noir. Cattier's pride and joy is a tiny walled plot within the commune of 2.2 hectares called Clos du Moulin from where they make their prestige cuvée. Like Taittinger's Comtes de Champagne, it is always a blend of three vintages. They also make a Blanc des Blancs from the Montagne, which makes for an interesting contrast to the classic Côte des Blancs style of chardonnay.

In 2000 Cattier set out to create the world's most expensive champagne – **Armand de Brignac** – in a gold-plated bottle. Having launched it six years later, the so-called Ace of Spades quickly hit the headlines thanks to the rapper Jay Z (Shawn Carter) spotting it glinting in his local New York wine shop. Within no time he was rapping about "this Spade shit", around the time he was dissing Louis Roederer's Cristal. Jay-Z went on to acquire the brand still produced by Cattier and before long was making "a little over US$4 million" a year from it according to the writer Zack O'Malley Greenburg. LVMH now own 50% of the brand and handle the distribution. Recently, magnums of the first vintage expression from 2015 were released for the princely sum of £2,650.

Considerably more affordable is the highly rated champagne **Bruno Paillard**, founded by the current chairman and CEO of Lanson-BCC – the biggest brand-owner after LVMH. Coming from an ancient family of growers, Paillard learned his trade as a broker. Most of what he sourced disappeared into supermarket own-label champagne, but particularly good parcels were kept aside and sold under his name. Having built a prototype brand, he became the first person in modern times to establish a champagne House from scratch in 1981. The wines are food-friendly and built to last with pinot noir the lead grape, while the running of this boutique House is now in the hands of Bruno's daughter Alice.

Above (left): The cellars of Canard-Duchêne were once owned by LVMH, but it was bought out by Alain Thiénot in 2003.

Above: When it comes to bling and big-format bottles no one out-aces Armand de Brignac, whose 30 litre Midas bottles sell in nightclubs for six-figure sums.

Heading south from the Montagne de Reims you hit the ancient champagne village of Aÿ. It was here that William Deutz worked for Bollinger before setting up his own House next door in 1838. Champagne **Deutz** suffered in the riots of 1911 when its cellar was destroyed, but survived in family hands until the early 1990s when Louis Roederer bought it. Today Deutz owns 42 of the 200 hectares of *premier* and *Grand Cru* vineyards it sources grapes from, all in the Marne valley and within 20 miles of Aÿ. Its new owners have more than trebled production to more than two million bottles, yet under the dynamic leadership of Roederer's Fabrice Rosset, the champagne's reputation seems as high as ever.

The riots also claimed Château d'Aÿ, which was burnt to the ground only to be rebuilt two years later. The original château was a wedding gift to Edmond de Ayala, a Colombian diplomat, from his father-in-law the Viscount of Mareuil, along with some esteemed vineyards. Champagne **Ayala** was founded soon after, in 1860, and later became the favourite fizz of King George VI. Its reputation had all but collapsed by 2005 when rescued by its neighbour, Bollinger. Under its new owners the focus has been on Ayala's bone-dry house style, notably its crisp, sugar-free Brut Nature. There is also a well-regarded Blanc des Blancs and a prestige cuvée called Perle d'Ayala.

The Swiss de Venoge family was linked to the neighbouring village of Dizy before Henri-Marc de Venoge returned from Switzerland with his Italian wife to found Champagne **De Venoge** in 1837. While his son Joseph helped develop the business in France and Belgium, his other son Léon did the same in the US having emigrated there. De Venoge launched its Cordon Bleu brand in 1851, some 25 years before Mumm's rather more famous Cordon Rouge hit the shelves. By then third-generation Gaëtan de Venoge had been one of the founders of the Syndicat des Grandes Marques. Over time the family connection petered out and the House eventually became part of the Lanson-BCC group. In 2014 it was announced that it would be moving into Maison Gallice, one of the grandest Houses in Épernay's Avenue de Champagne.

Four years before Maison Gallice was built in 1899, the Viscount Florens de Castellane launched his Champagne House. With its St Andrew's cross in bold red, Champagne **De Castellane** sought to stand out from rivals with a mere single sash like Mumm and De Venoge on their labels. And its HQ towered above its rivals in Épernay with its striped brick tower that still offers a commanding view of the town. Today De Castellane is part of the Laurent-Perrier empire.

One other Champagne House to mention in Épernay is **Alfred Gratien**, founded in 1867 by a man who believed "champagne should be to wine what haute couture is to fashion". His descendants eventually sold out to Henkell & Söhnlein in 2004, which caused some alarm going from family-ownership to that of Germany's biggest Sekt producer. However Nicolas Jaeger was retained as *chef de cave* and as the fourth generation of his family to hold the post, there is a great sense of continuity at Alfred Gratien. The firm have been supplying the Wine Society with their well-regarded house champagne since 1906.

Just to the west, in Damery, **Telmont** has been reinvigorated by Ludovic du Plessis who is committed to making the most sustainable champagne possible with organic vines, recycled glass bottles and renewable energy. Heading south on the D10 from Épernay you pass through the fabled villages of the Côte des Blancs. The fact this is chardonnay country is epitomised by the boutique house of **Salon**. Aimé Salon released the first bottles in 1911 with the sole purpose of expressing this one grape variety from a single Grand Cru village, Le Mesnil-sur-Oger, from a particular vintage with no blending involved. The House itself was founded after the First World, and has been releasing its vintage wines four or five times a decade on average. It was the legendary '28 Salon that Bernard de Nonacourt discovered as a young tank commander in Hitler's secret cellar in a cave in the Bavarian Alps in 1945.

After the war, de Nonancourt took over Laurent-Perrier and finally bought Salon in 1999. Laurent-Perrier also acquired Salon's stable-mate and fellow chardonnay devotee, Champagne **Delamotte**, the fifth oldest Champagne House, founded in 1760 in Le Mesnil.

Just nearby, in the premier cru village of Vertus, is **Duval-Leroy**, the only *Grande Maison* in the Côte des Blancs, which, from the sight of its futuristic, solar-panelled winery you would never guess was founded back in 1859. It is still family-run and now in its sixth generation with 200 hectares of mainly chardonnay. When her husband died young in 1991, Carol Duval-Leroy was aged just 39 with a business to run and three young boys to bring up. She proved every bit as dynamic as those famed champagne widows before her. The House is now managed by her son Julien with the strapline 'inspired by passion not fashion' which sounds like a gentle riposte to LVMH. Its chardonnay-led prestige cuvée – Femme de Champagne is only released in the best years.

As you head on down to the Côte des Bar, chardonnay gives way to pinot noir thanks to the pioneering work of men like Georges Collot of **Drappier**, who was dubbed *père pinot* (father pinot) for his efforts to replace the discredited gamay grape that once dominated the vineyards. One of Drappier's pure pinot noir champagnes was the favourite of Charles de Gaulle when he retired to the nearby village of Colombey-les-Deux-Églises. Today Georges' grandson Michel Drappier heads up the House that owns 62 hectares and has control of a further 50, making it the most important producer in the region. Drappier has been based in Urville since 1803 and ages its champagne in the magnificent vaulted cellars of the twelfth-century Clairvaux Abbey. Its flagship wine is Carte d'Or, which is at least 80% pinot noir, while its top expression is the single vineyard Grande Sendrée that also comes as a rosé.

Opposite (left): Founded by a Colombian diplomat in 1860, Ayala had a reputation in need of considerable TLC when rescued by the neighbouring House of Bollinger in 2005.

Opposite (right): Set up by William Deutz in the village of Aÿ in 1838, Champagne Deutz is now owned by Louis Roederer.

Opposite (left): Since Carol Duval-Leroy took over the family House in 1991, annual production has grown to 5.5 million bottles.

Below: Champagne De Venoge was founded in 1837 by Henri-Marc de Venoge from Switzerland. Today it is part of the Lanson-BCC group.

Overleaf: The sun breaks through the clouds over the patchwork vineyards of the Vallée de la Marne.

CHAMPAGNE COOPERATIVES

The idea of the local cooperative winery crushing the grapes of all its growers, fermenting the juice in a giant stainless-steel tank and bottling the result, doesn't necessarily suggest quality. All over Europe, and probably in this region as well, there are cooperatives where there is no real attempt to be selective in the blind pursuit of volume. Yet, in champagne, there are a surprising number of really good cooperatives, whose winemakers appear to be every bit as passionate and skilled as those of the Grandes Marques. Their wines consistently shine in blind tastings, and stand out on the shelf for their relative good value.

Take **Mailly Grand Cru**, a cooperative set up in 1929 to protect the growers in this leading village on the northern flank of the Montagne de Reims during the Depression. It was established by Gabriel Simon with 24 founding members, and you can gauge their commitment by the fact they began digging out the cooperative's chalk cellars by hand, a task that took 40 years. Today there are more than 80 members who own 74 hectares between them, or one-third of all Mailly's Grand Cru vineyards. Here on the northern fringes of planet wine, the received wisdom is that you need to blend from a wider area if you want to make good wine every year. But in Mailly, as in the village of Aÿ, it seems there is enough variety in the slopes and topography to hedge against vintage variation. With some 500 parcels of mainly top-quality pinot noir, the winemaker has a great spectrum of wines to create the blends.

While Mailly Grand Cru sells 90% of its production under its label, a far more typical scenario for a cooperative is that of Champagne **Palmer**, which sells 70% of its fruit to the Champagne Houses, keeping the best for itself. It was founded by seven growers after the Second World War and now has more than 200 members with over 400 hectares in total spread across 40 villages. The vineyards are mainly grand and premier cru in the Montagne de Reims. No one quite knows where the English name came from, though it may have been inspired by Huntley & Palmer. Apparently the Champenois considered them the *crème de la crème* of biscuits after the war. Today it is one of the top-rated smaller cooperatives, with annual sales of half a million bottles.

This is dwarfed by **Jacquart**, the flagship brand of the Alliance Group, an amalgam of three big cooperatives, established in 1994, which now has a total of 1,800 members. Jacquart itself dates from the early 1960s with just 30 growers involved at the start. That number has since blossomed to around 700, covering 1,000 hectares in 64 different villages. Today more than three million bottles of Jacquart are produced

with strong sales in the UK, the USA and Japan. In the cellar is the talented young winemaker Floriane Eznack, who joined in 2010 from Veuve Clicquot, while one-third of production is of Jacquart's popular Mosaique Brut NV.

The biggest player in the Côte des Blancs is the Union Champagne in Avize, with no fewer than 13 cooperatives under its umbrella and a production equivalent to 12 million bottles. Between them the members own 1,200 hectares, nearly all in top-rated villages, mostly planted with chardonnay in the Côte des Blancs, but with some pinot noir in the Montagne de Reims as well. The cooperative sells around 2.5 million bottles under its own labels, principally **De Saint Gall**, which has done well in the UK supermarkets. The rest is sold off to the likes of Moët & Chandon, Taittinger and Piper Heidsieck. These Houses are prepared to pay top dollar for the best grapes, which might find their way into Dom Pérignon or Taittinger's Comtes de Champagnes for example.

Down the road in Le Mesnil-sur-Oger, home to Krug's legendary Clos du Mesnil Blanc de Bancs, is Champagne **Le Mesnil**, a very upmarket cooperative with around 300 hectares of east-facing slopes in this famous Grand Cru. With a tiny average holding, the 553 members farm their plots like allotments, while the cooperative sells all but 8% of its production to the big Champagne Houses. It sells little more than 120,000 bottles under its own label.

The giant **Nicolas Feuillatte** could not be more different. It is the flagship brand of Terroirs et Vignerons de Champagne (TEVC), an amalgam of 82 cooperatives which represent nearly 6000 wine-growers across 2750 hectares. With global sales of over 10 million bottles it claims to be third to Top of the Pops Moët & Chandon and Veuve Clicquot and the best-seller in French supermarkets. The original M. Feuillatte, who died in 2014, made a fortune from the post-war instant coffee boom in the States before buying 12 hectares in Champagne and launching his wine in 1976. He sold it to the cooperative 10 years later, but continued as its brand ambassador, particularly in the USA. Feuillatte's massive, shiny

HQ in the village of Chouilly stands in stark contrast to the palatial, *fin de siècle* mansions of the Champagne House in Épernay and Reims. And there is no attempt to conceal the scale of the operation, with visitors whisked on airport-style conveyor belts past giant vats of gleaming stainless steel.

All this was a far cry from the genteel world of Claude-Joseph Devaux, who found herself widowed and in charge of a Champagne House in Épernay in 1846. No fewer than three widows ran **Champagne Devaux**, the last one dying in 1951, but the name lives on as the highly rated brand of the main cooperative in the Aube. Formerly known as the Union Auboise and run by the dynamic Laurent Gillet, it has 800 growers and 1,384 hectares of primarily pinot noir vineyards.

Opposite: Set up in 1929, the Mailly Grand Cru cooperative now has 74 hectares of vineyards owned and farmed by 70 members.

Above (left): The imposing head office of Jacquart, the flagship brand of the giant Alliance Group of cooperatives that now has around 1,800 members.

Above (right): A poster from the 1920s advertising Champagne Devaux, then privately owned, now the brand of the biggest cooperative in the Aube.

GROWER CHAMPAGNES

With more than 2,000 grower producers, or *récoltant-manipulants,* to choose from, visiting Champagne can be totally bewildering with its profusion of unknown names. How much simpler is the UK high street, with its selection of tried and tested brands and a scattering of cheaper own-label alternatives. Here are just a few grower champagnes, in alphabetical order, worth looking out for ...

The **Agrapart** family in Avize have been doing it longer than most, and brothers Pascal and Fabrice are fourth-generation grower-producers. With 10 hectares in their home village and Oger, Cramant and Oiry, the vineyards are as natural as can be, though not certified organic or biodynamic. The vines are well into middle age, with some pushing 70 years old, and the wines are all aged on their lees for at least three years, seven in the case of vintage bottlings. Pascal Agrapart has been hailed a genius in the cellar, though he shrugs it off, giving credit to the terroir and the vagaries of the weather.

To the north in the village of Bouzy, in the Montagne de Reims, you will find **Paul Bara** with a similar holding to that of the Agroparts. The family were growers in Bouzy and supplied the champagne Houses and then the local cooperative for more than a century, before they began bottling their wines in earnest after the Second World War. Old vine pinot noir is something of a speciality here, with wines like Bara's Grand Millésime, Comtesse Marie de France and Spécial Club.

Among the *récoltant-manipulants,* recognisable by their RM on the label, there are no shortage of mavericks like Yannick Doyard, whose stylish, characterful wines have won a loyal following. Within his production of just over 50,000 bottles, you can find an old-style *oeil de perdrix* rosé and a special cuvée – La Libertine – with 60g/l of sugar, enough to satisfy even the most sweet-toothed Russian from the nineteenth century.

Also with vines in Bouzy, but mainly in Ambonnay and Verzenay, is Francis Egly, whose **Egly-Ouriet** champagnes are among the most prized in the whole of the Montagne de Reims. These include a pure pinot meunier called *Les Vignes de Vrigny* and a fabled Blanc de Noirs *Vielles Vignes.* With naturally low yields, just 12 hectares and a voracious fan club, new releases sell out fast, as does the still wine Ambonnay Rouge. Meanwhile the **Gimonnet** family from Cuis in the Côte des Blancs boast nearly 30 hectares and a history as growers stretching back to the mid-eighteenth century. They finally got round to selling the wine under the name Pierre Gimonnet in 1935. With vines now averaging around 50 years in age, the yields are slightly lower and the fruit that bit riper, meaning Didier and Olivier Gimonnet don't have to chaptalise their wines, unlike most producers in Champagne. Like Bollinger they keep some of their reserve wines in bottle.

In Bollinger's home village of Aÿ, the family of **Henri Goutorbe** were best known for their nursery, set up during the First World War to help replant the vineyards after phylloxera. It was a thriving business by all accounts and allowed the family to accumulate just over 20 hectares in Aÿ and neighbouring villages. With their sumptuous pinot noir fruit, the Goutorbes make a classy Brut Cuvée Tradition NV and Prestige 1er Cru, and a spectacular Spécial Club Grand Cru. All the wines are aged for at least three years on the lees.

At **Larmandier-Bernier**, winemaker Pierre Larmandier has been treading a biodynamic path since 2000 with much of the wine fermented in oak with wild yeast. The family own 19 hectares of the Côte des Blancs in villages like Oger, Avize and Cramant, and have built up a glowing reputation for their crisp, mineral, low-dosage wines with chardonnay in the lead, or solo, role.

To the north, in the village of Gueus near Reims, the 2.2 hectares of pinot meunier inherited by Jérôme Prévost in 1987 would hardly seem the basis to go it alone as a *récoltant-manipulant*. But that's precisely what he did with the encouragement of Anselme Selosse some 10 years later. Today his intense, spicy, barrel-fermented wines have developed a cult following.

Labelled **Jacques Selosse**, and now run by Anselms's son Guillaume, the wines come from the family's low-cropped vineyards in Avize, Cramant and Oger, to which have been added small plots in Aÿ, Ambonnay and Mareuil. Everything is fermented in second-hand casks from some of the top estates in Burgundy and have an uncompromisingly earthy style that divides opinion. Some say they are overblown and oxidised, others love them with a passion. Either way they feel like a riposte to the big names out there with their consistent house styles and lifestyle marketing campaigns.

A few years after Selosse, the late **Erick De Sousa** took the plunge to become a *récoltant-manipulant* in 1986 with nine hectares of Grand Cru vineyards in Avize, Oger, Le Mesnil-sur-Oger, Chouilly and Grauves. The vines are farmed biodynamically, and tractors have given way to horses. Like a number of leading growers, he made his top cuvée des Caudalies, in a *solera* system whereby the casks are refreshed with a new vintage each year to add a nutty, oaked character to the wines. Erick died in 2023, leaving his three children in charge.

Finally to **Vilmart**, a grower champagne from the picturesque village of Rilly-la-Montagne in the Montagne de Reims which has been around since 1890, though its fame is much more recent. Laurent Champs, the fifth generation, has been carefully crafting the wines since 1989 including the complex, rich, subtly-oaked Coeur de Cuvée that is four-fifths chardonnay. Though not quite in the same league, their 'basic' pinot noir-led Grande Réserve is pretty impressive too.

Opposite (left): The family of Henri Goutorbe have accumulated 20 hectares of vineyards in Aÿ and its neighbouring villages since being set up during the First World War.

Opposite (right): Champagnes made by the grower Jacques Selosse are known for dividing opinion. They are fermented in second-hand casks from some of the top estates in Burgundy.

Above: (left) The spent lees in a bottle of Erick de Sousa's champagne. This grower-producer began in 1986 and produces his cuvée de caudalies in a sherry-style solera system.

Above: (right) *Coeur de Cuvée*, a champagne produced by Vilmart, ages in a cellar. It was first created by René and Laurent Champs in 1989.

SPARKLING WINES OF THE WORLD

It has been champagne's genius to rise above the sea of mere 'sparkling wine' and present itself as something unique – often copied but never equalled. Of course, the price and prestige of its wines have only encouraged others to try using the same methods and grapes. When tasted blind, some of these champagne lookalikes can be virtually indistinguishable from the real thing, while others are happy to be just frothy, frivolous and fun.

PROSECCO

At the start of the third millennium few people outside of Italy and Germany had heard of prosecco, which suddenly exploded in Britain. Dubbed 'recession champagne' during the financial crash of 2008, its appeal has proved to be much more enduring.

Shortly after the financial crash, the charity Arts & Business was hosting its annual awards party. "When you are cutting your workforce and seeing your profits slide, the last thing you want to be seen doing is throwing champagne at some classy event," said its CEO Colin Tweedy, on the eve of its event. "It'll be the pop of a prosecco cork at this year's awards," he added. "No champagne I'm afraid."

Being inappropriate in times of an economic downturn is one of the downsides for champagne, with its glamourous and not exactly humble image. And yet it barely begins to explain the meteoric rise of prosecco whose global sales overtook champagne in around 2014 and are now over 700 million bottles a year. Clearly the sparkler from the Veneto in north-east Italy is more than just a cheap alternative to champagne when times are tough.

Like almost all sparkling wines, prosecco was inspired by champagne in the late nineteenth century when Antonio Carpenè treated his local white wine to some bottle fermentation. He was a professor of chemistry and in 1876 founded Italy's first school of oenology in the town of Conegliano, north of Venice. Some 20 years later, in north-west Italy a winemaker called Federico Martinotti patented a new, far simpler way of making sparkling wine.

Martinotti thought that instead of fiddling around with a prolonged secondary fermentation in bottles, which then have to be riddled, disgorged and topped up as in Champagne, why not do the whole process in a sealed tank? The tank would be injected with yeast and kept under pressure to preserve the CO_2 in the wine. Tank fermentation, also known as the Charmat method or *Metodo Martinotti*, came to define Italian sparkling wine be it Asti Spumante or prosecco.

The 'P' word first appeared on a label when Antonio Carpenè's son, Etile, began to market a '*Prosecco Amabile dei Colli di Conegliano*' in 1924. And yet for the next 50 years it was a slow burn for this local wine which hung out in bars from Verona to Venice and was drunk as a simple *brindisi*, or toast. Few if anyone in Champagne had ever heard of prosecco.

The first foreigners to embrace the wine were the Germans, who discovered it on holiday and brought the taste back home where it began to rival sales of home-grown Sekt. While the Brits needed a special occasion to crack open a bottle of sparkling wine, the Germans would be popping corks at any excuse so long as it was cheap. This was to lead to a big bust-up in the land of prosecco.

The original wine was Prosecco DOC from the conical hills around Conegliano and Valdobiadenne, just north of Treviso, while the fizz produced on the Venetian plain, with fewer regulations, was categorised as Prosecco IGT. These semantics mattered greatly to the producers up in the hills, who were appalled at what was happening down on the flatlands. The generous maximum yields permitted under the IGT rules were being routinely flouted and bulk exports were being mixed with God knows what to hit prices as low as €1.50 a bottle in German supermarkets.

The final straw was when an Austrian entrepreneur launched a canned version called Rich Prosecco in 2006, and hired Paris Hilton to promote

Above: Antonio Carpenè, the founding father of prosecco, whose pioneering efforts were made in champagne's image. Tank-fermented prosecco came later.

Opposite: A bunch of glera, which anyone can grow outside the land of Prosecco in north-east Italy and produce sparkling wine. The only rule is that they mustn't use the P-word.

it in the nude sprayed with gold paint in a stunt ripped from James Bond in the film *Goldfinger*. When she appeared on the *Late Show with David Letterman* in the US, Ms Hilton explained that prosecco was Italian champagne. "Italian champagne? In a can? Champagne in a can!?" spluttered Letterman. "It's sexy," came the reply. "It looks great when you're holding it." Whether viewers were convinced seems unlikely.

"*Basta*!" (enough!) cried the Italians, who were suddenly galvanized into action. Prosecco IGT became a DOC that stretched from Trieste to Verona, while the original DOC was upgraded to Prosecco Superiore DOCG. Yields were reduced, bulk exports were banned and crucially the prosecco grape was rechristened glera – presumably the ugliest synonym the producers could find. A small village was discovered near Trieste called Prosecco, which somehow allowed the whole area to protect itself like Champagne. Anyone wishing to produce it outside the region was invited to call it glera or face the full might of Italian law. So far, but for Brazilian and Australian prosecco sold locally, the Italians have been largely successful.

Having secured its borders, prosecco has surged in the USA and the UK – its two biggest markets, followed by Germany and now France. Being tank-fermented and made from a different grape, the beauty of prosecco is that it is not trying to be champagne. It is frothy and frivolous and every day. In the words of Massimo Tuzzi, the former boss of Zonin, one of the big producers: "If prosecco were a dress code it would be 'smart casual', as opposed to 'black tie' for champagne." Being softer, with a degree less alcohol, it is a touch more forgiving the morning after, and its relative sweetness being mainly Extra-Dry as opposed to Brut like virtually all champagne is another reason for its popularity.

Across the region, there was a huge replanting of vineyards to reach a current total of 28,000 hectares for Prosecco DOC, to compliment the 8,600 ha used to produce some 90 million bottles of Prosecco Superiore. The latter tries valiantly to distance itself from its namesake, pointing out that its steep slopes have to be tended by hand, unlike the heavily mechanised vineyards of the plain. Processing the grapes costs 30% more per kilo than champagne, it has been claimed.

The prosecco boom "has brought so much awareness to the region," says the English master of wine Sarah Abbott about the hills of the DOCG. "It has increased land values and meant young people can stay on the family farm. But on the other hand, most UK consumers do not know what good prosecco is really about." In her words: "youthful elegance is the soul of good prosecco."

Pink prosecco now accounts for a tenth of sales, and its leading brand in the UK has been one from Kylie Minogue, with wine supplied by Zonin. Other recent celebrity tie-ups include Dolly Parton, but for all its popularity, prosecco remains fairly generic. Its somewhat promiscuous consumers flip from one prosecco to another, depending on what's on offer. Unlike the famous names of champagne, there is little brand loyalty. While at the bottom end, bulk fizz has been resurfacing as "prosecco on tap" in the UK, prompting the wine's Consorzio to launch a campaign on the London Underground."This is not Prosecco," shouted posters, featuring a steel keg. "Do not call it Prosecco. It is a common effervescent wine."

Opposite: The wine's heartland, classified as Prosecco Superiore DOCG, lies in the conical hills north of Treviso.

Below (left): Secondary fermentation takes just 30 days in pressurised stainless steel tanks.

Below (right): Zonin, Italy's largest privately owned wine business, is determined to build a strong brand that stands out from the sea of generic prosecco.

CAVA AND OTHER SPARKLING WINES

Before prosecco burst onto the scene, cava was the principle alternative fizz for those on a budget. Like other bottle-fermented wines it was made just like champagne, albeit from different grapes. Today virtually every wine-producing nation, including India, makes a sparkling wine.

While the Italians were inventing sparkling prosecco, Josep Raventos returned from his European travels to create a Spanish sparkling wine to rival champagne at his family's winery of Codorníu in Penedès in 1872. This was the first of what became cava – the Spanish word for cellar, yet for some time it advertised itself as 'Champagne Codorníu'. Other producers soon joined in, selling their brands of Spanish champagne.

For much of the twentieth century, champagne producers considered it a brazen attempt to surf on the back of their fame and fortune, while the Spanish and others making sparkling wine argued that the 'C' word had become pretty well generic. As we know, it was a battle the French eventually won, even succeeding in banning the term '*méthode champenoise*' within the EU in 1994 because no-one could agree a definition. Cava has been known as such since the 1970s, since when it is fair to say it has never really been associated with luxury fizz.

For something made in champagne's image, it now finds itself in the ignominious position of competing toe to toe with tank-fermented prosecco. Indeed, despite the added costs of bottle fermentation for a minimum of nine months on the lees, cava is often discounted below the price of the Italian upstart.

Cava is traditionally produced from three local white grapes, with xarello said to provide the structure, parellada adding a certain creamy texture and macabeo giving freshness and acidity. That said, these are fairly neutral varieties, especially when picked early. Since 1959, the wine has had its own *Denominacion de Origin* (DO), or appellation, which now allows chardonnay in the blend, while the black grapes for pink *cava rosado* include pinot noir, garnacha and cabernet sauvignon.

In theory, the area of production is huge and covers eight regions from Rioja in the north-east to Extremadura in the west. In practice, cava is very much a Catalan wine, with around 95% coming from the Penedès region, just down the coast from Barcelona. The epicentre is the town

of Sant Sadurní d'Anoia in the Alt Penedès which is home to the mighty Codorníu and Freixenet. A price war between these two brands, a surfeit of own-label cava in the supermarkets, and a somewhat coarse, yeasty character in some of the cheap stuff, conspired to drive down the wine's image.

Some 250 million bottles of cava are sold worldwide every year, around 30% of them in Spain. In 2020 new regulations were introduced by the cava regulatory council with the hope of improving quality and provenance. The production zone now has to be mentioned on the label, including the five sub-zones in Penedès, and ageing requirements have been tightened up with a minimum nine months for basic 'Cava Guarda'. The upper 'Superiore' level has a minimum of 18 months for Reserva and 30 months for Gran Reserva, while above that Cava de Paraje Calificado, must be aged for at least 36 months like vintage champagne.

There are plenty of quality-orientated producers, but they often struggle to stand out from the mass of cheap, commoditized cava. This has led to various breakaway movements like Corpinnat whose members come from a specified area of Penedès, grow their vines organically and age their wines for at least 18 months. As Xavier Gramona, one of the producers

Opposite: Bush-trained vines in the dry heat of Penedès.

Above: Bottles of Cordoníu waiting to be riddled by hand. In reality the process is all done mechanically by industrial *gyropalettes* well out of sight of any tourists.

Below (right): A cava-powered vehicle promoting Codorníu's great rival.

involved, explained: "We don't want to abandon the DO, but we need to add value so that the 5,000 farmers who work in the sector can survive. In Champagne, a farmer with five hectares drives a Mercedes. Here, he can hardly make ends meet."

But the tide may be turning for cava, whose quality has slowly improved in recent decades. Being grown in a relatively warm climate compared to most sparkling wine, there is less need for added sugar to balance the wine, and less need for pesticides in the vineyards. Indeed, within Penedès, every drop now has to be made from organically-grown grapes. Stylistically cava tends to be bone dry without the hint of richness you can find in champagne, but the Spanish believe that makes it a good match for food.

Back in France, sparkling wine extends far beyond champagne with bottle-fermented alternatives typically called crémant, as in Crémant de Loire, Crémant d'Alsace and Crémant de Limoux from the foothills of the Pyrenees. The latter was known as Blanquette de Limoux or originally Vin de Blanquette and claims to be the oldest sparkling wine in the world. It was a sweet, cloudy wine produced by the monks of the Abbaye de Saint-Hilaire that may have had bubbles when it first appeared in 1531. It is a now a crystal clear, dry sparkler that is still made from the local mauzac grape.

Moving to Germany, a vast ocean of sparkling Sekt is produced, the vast majority tank-fermented from all manner of grapes unless called *Deutscher Sekt*, in which case the grapes have to be German. When made from Riesling, "the wines tend to be fresh, slightly floral, with plenty of apple and lime fruit flavours, and depending on the amount of time the fizz spends in contact with its lees, a touch of breadiness too," claims the drinks writer and master of wine, Patrick Schmitt. At the other end of the scale is cheap German *Schaumwein*, literally 'foam wine', made from injecting Co2 as though via a soda stream and best avoided.

The Italians offer a number of bottle-fermented sparklers alongside prosecco and Asti spumante, of which the most famous is Franciacorta. This small appellation of 2,200 hectares lies between the northern city of Padua and the Lago d'Iseo. There have been local vineyards since Roman times, but the wine was still – until Franco Ziliani, winemaker at Berlucchi, created what was originally called Pinot di Franciacorta in 1961. Today production has been capped at 17.6 million bottles a year, and most is consumed in Lombardy, especially in Milan. The wine has to be aged for a minimum of 18 months on the lees, rising to 60 months for the Riserva, and the grapes must be at least half pinot noir and chardonnay, and no more than half pinot blanc. Today it is rivalled by Trentodoc, a champagne look-alike from the foothills of the Dolomites, whose biggest brand is Ferrari. It's a nice name to have, but actually predates Enzo Ferrari and his four-wheeled version by 27 years.

The trouble with being a champagne look-alike is that it is hard to shake off the idea that you are a tribute band to 'the real thing' back in France. Of course, this was no issue for the big Champagne Houses and their satellite operations that began with Moët & Chandon's Bodegas Chandon in Argentina, followed by Domaine Chandon in California in the 1970s. While there was always a risk that some Moët drinkers might be lost to these New World brand extensions, there was plenty of scope to recruit an army of new consumers. That it worked out was testament to the power of champagne, and before long other producers like Mumm, Roederer and Pommery were heading to the Sunshine State to set up their own outposts.

When some pesky wine critics put Mumm champagne to the test in a blind tasting with its cheaper Cuvée Napa alternative and concluded the Californian version was better, the French were unimpressed. "Personally," sniffed one of the leading *champenoise*, "I wouldn't compare blondes with brunettes." In 1986, Moët & Chandon took over an old dairy farm in Australia's Yarra valley called Green Point, though this time their venture was not copied by other Champagne Houses. The Australians have a vibrant sparkling wine industry of their own, particularly in Tasmania. In New Zealand there are now more than 100 producers of bottle-fermented fizz, particularly in Marlborough whose sauvignon vineyards were originally planted with that in mind. Today most New Zealand sparkling wine is from the classic trio of champagne grapes.

Above (left): Ferrari sparkling wine has been the official F1 celebration wine since 2021.

Above (right) : Moët & Chandon was the first Champagne House to open a satellite operation in the Napa Valley in 1973.

Below (right): The Yarra Valley, near Melbourne, has been home to Domaine Chandon – Moët & Chandon's Australian satellite – since 1986.

Overleaf: Based in the Catalan town of Sant Sadurní d'Anoia – the epicentre of Cava production, Freixenet claims to be the world's largest producer of bottle-fermented fizz.

CAVAS
FREIXENET

ENGLISH FIZZ

The story of champagne's origins as an Anglo-French co-production (see pages 30–31) with the French providing the base wine and the English the strong glass and a bit of sugar has, to some extent, come full circle.

In late 2015, news broke that Taittinger was to become the first Champagne House to make English sparkling wine, having bought a former Kent apple orchard in partnership with its UK agent, Hatch Mansfield. Forty hectares were planted with chardonnay, pinot noir and pinot meunier to make Domaine Evremond, named after the French, ex-pat bon viveur who promoted champagne, albeit probably without bubbles, at the court of King Charles II.

The story had been a hardy perennial of the UK press – the sight of Frenchmen prospecting for vineyards across the Channel driven there by fears of global warming in Champagne. The fact that they returned empty-handed was a detail glossed over in excited reports in the *Daily Mail*, until it happened for real. At around the same time, Vranken-Pommery acquired the 40-hectare Pinglestone estate in Hampshire and began planting vines. A winery was added a few years later.

In the end Pommery sailed past Taittinger to release its Louis Pommery English Brut in 2020. The name refers to the House's co-founder, whose story had been somewhat buried beneath that of his famous widow, Louise, and there was already a Louis Pommery Brut California. The English version is now widely available and is to be joined by a Pingelstone Estate sparkling wine.

Domaine Evremond was finally launched in early 2025, having unveiled its new winery on an inauspiciously wet day the previous autumn. "This is a huge, historic emblem of friendship between the English and the French," declared Vitalie Taittinger. Some years earlier

her father, Pierre-Emmanuel, was asked the inevitable question of whether English sparkling wine would ever rival champagne. "When things are good, we don't talk about nationality," he replied. "Mozart is Mozart. Alec Guinness is Alec Guinness. Brigitte Bardot is Brigitte Bardot."

It was a wonderfully Gallic response, yet producers of English fizz love nothing better than submitting to blind tastings and beating the French at their own game. It was in the late 1990s that a bottle of Nyetimber Classic Cuvée ran off with the IWSC trophy for the world's best sparkling wine, including champagne. The estate in West Sussex had been planted with the three champagne grapes by its owners, Sandy and Stuart Moss from Chicago, who had ignored advice to grow apples instead. For Julia Trustram-Eve, the former head of marketing at WineGB and now an independent consultant for the sector, "That's when people really sat up and took notice."

But getting to that point has been quite a journey, considering the Romans were the first to plant vines in England, and that there were as many as 42 vineyards recorded in the Doomsday Book of 1085. After the 'Medieval warm period', things turned decidedly chilly and the northern fringes of planet wine began to retreat back to France, while imported wine became cheaper and more available.

By the 1950s English wine had become an eccentric hobby, and in some cases a joke. Using Germanic hybrid varieties bred for a cold climate, it was a way to prove that you could make fermented grape juice, though whether you should was not always obvious.

It tended to be still wine, whereas the proximity of Champagne clearly suggested it would be worth trying to make it sparkling. The need for a relatively neutral, acidic base wine was something a reasonable summer in southern England could achieve in most years. Another clue lay in the ground, because the same band of chalk that breaks through the surface of the Côte des Blancs in Champagne reappears in the white cliffs of Dover and on the South Downs.

If you select the right slope on the right soil, which is as sun-drenched and sheltered as possible, and match it with the most suitable clones of chardonnay, pinot noir and pinot meunier, you are in with a chance of producing a good sparkling wine. Not that you have to use the champagne grapes, as Peter Hall more than proved with Seyval Blanc, which he first planted at Breaky Bottom in East Sussex in 1974.

There were then perhaps half a dozen vineyards in the entire country. Today there are over a thousand covering 4,000 hectares, with the most northerly just beyond York. Production in 2023 was enough to fill 22 million bottles of wine, of which three quarters was sparkling. Within a decade the area under vine is predicted to reach 7,600 ha – over a quarter of Champagne. For now, wine is the UK's fastest-growing industry within agriculture.

Leading producers include Wiston Estates, Hattingley Valley, Sugrue South Downs, Ridgeview, Chapel Down, Langham... but the list grows ever longer. Global warming is clearly a factor, but it's not the only one.

Opposite: Founded in 2008, Hampshire's Hattingley Valley released its first wine five years later.

Above (left): Hambledon is England's oldest commercial vineyard.

Above (right): Nyetimber's victory in the IWSR awards as the 'world's best sparkling wine' in 1993, was a defining moment for English fizz.

To suggest that Tunbridge Wells is the new Épernay, as one English producer has, is stretching the truth. The South Coast may be close as the crow flies, but its climate is temperate and maritime compared to the more continental weather system in Champagne. Similarly, while many producers wax lyrical about their chalky soil, there are plenty of good vineyards planted on sand and clay.

Farmers in southern England blessed with the right plots and protected from the wind may be dreaming of replanting that field of turnips and perhaps one day producing a nectar to rival Krug or Dom Pérignon. Not that it's easy to produce a consistent wine there, and in some years it may be too wet to pick any grapes at all.

In his book *Ancient Land, Pastures New*, Christopher Coates chronicled the highs and lows of his boutique winery in Berkshire through rain, shine, frost and more rain. For him one thing that sets English sparkling wine apart is a "preference for fruit-forward fizz versus long lees ageing," he says. "The English tend to disgorge after 24 months so as not to lose the fruit whereas the French leave longer to get that biscuity, brioche, often at the expense of fruit." The Champenoise might dispute that last point.

The gentle curve of the planet – the fact that daylight hours are slightly longer through the summer months – helps offset the slightly lower temperatures to allow winemaking at all this side of the Channel. And who knows, it may add something to the freshness and quality

of the fruit. The average growing season is around ten days longer in southern England, and closer to the hundred days that was once the norm in Champagne.

These subtle differences will be important as English sparkling wine forges its own identity. For now, it can be very hard to tell a good example apart from Champagne when tasted blind. Inevitably people will compare Pommery English Brut with the Pommery mother-brand, just as they will do with Taittinger and Domaine Evremond.

"English sparkling wine is up there with the best from around the world," says Julia Trustram-Eve. "It's earned its own category. It's broken through onto the shelves of retailers up and down the country and on restaurant lists. Another route to market is through the successful and growing wine tourism trend in UK vineyards, with 200 vineyards across the country now open to visitors which is forging greater recognition and brand awareness."

So far, there has not been a stampede of French producers heading north on the heels of Pommery and Taittinger to plant vineyards here. A more likely scenario is the acquisition of an existing English winery by one of the big players in Champagne.

Whether the sector can keep expanding at the same rate remains to be seen, but the opportunity is certainly there. In 2018 the University of East Anglia published a report mapping out the whole of England and Wales in 50m² plots to identify the best vineyard sites. Nearly 35,000 hectares of potential "prime viticultural land" were identified. Essex and Sussex were considered to be "particularly promising." This neatly matches the 34,500 hectares planted in Champagne, though English production per hectare tends to be around half the French average.

Opposite (top): English vineyards could spread exponentially and may one day rival the 34,500 hectares planted in Champagne.

Opposite (below): The same strata of chalk that breaks through the topsoil in the Côte des Blancs in Champagne, resurfaces across the English Channel in the White Cliffs of Dover.

Above: Ridgeview's wines carry a dedication to Christopher Merret, who first documented the process of producing a traditional method sparkling wine in England in 1662.

Overleaf: Rows of vines at a Chapel Down's vineyard in Maidstone, UK.

5

CULTURE AND TRADITIONS

By the start of the twentieth century, nothing announced you had 'arrived' quite like the pop of a champagne cork. Writers, artists and film directors found the symbolism irresistible, whether to portray wealth, status, decadence or vice. Champagne has long been far more than just a drink.

"LIE BACK AND THINK OF FRANCE"

The Champagne House of E. Debray has long disappeared, but its name lives on in a gloriously effervescent poster by the artist Pierre Bonnard that was pasted all over Paris in the spring of 1891. The title, in bold, swirling capitals declares it is "France-champagne".

The poster depicts a curvy young woman, open-mouthed and eyes closed in ecstasy, clutching a glass overflowing with a frothing tide of fizz. Almost toppling out of her dress, if not the poster itself, she is the very essence of French *joie de vivre*.

The fame of champagne and its global success is clearly a source of pride to the French. It is the country's great sparkling ambassador around the world and offers a flattering reflection of the national psyche, brimming with wit and charm. For Voltaire: "The effervescence of this fresh wine reveals the true brilliance of the French people," while Bonnard's contemporary, Adolphe Brisson, claimed: "It is made in our image: it sparkles like our intellect." A little bombastic perhaps, even by French standards, but one imagines most Frenchmen would be suitably chuffed if you came to the same conclusion.

Of course, champagne does not reflect the whole of French society, only a part of it. In *When Champagne Became French*, Kolleen Guy includes a print from the time of the French Revolution called 'L'Accord fraternel' in which members of the Three Estates toast each other. The common man in his tricorn hat raises a glass of simple *vin rouge*. The clergyman does the same with some Burgundy, while a soldier, representing the aristocracy, lifts a dainty flute of champagne. This demonstrates plenty of *fraternité* and *liberté*, but not quite so much *égalité*. The truth is, champagne has always enjoyed an elite image as something to aspire to.

It wasn't the only product sold with added snob appeal. In her book, Guy unearths a lovely gem from the *Edinburgh Review* of 1834, advertising 'Mr Cockle's Antibilious Pills' as recommended by "ten dukes, five marquises, seventeen earls, eight viscounts, sixteen lords ..." and, presumably a partridge in a pear tree. Champagne brands battled to win those precious 'by appointment' contracts to European courts from Queen Victoria to the Russian Czars. At the same time the brand-owners were marrying off their daughters to the *ancien régime* and acquiring titles along the way. Concerns that the merchants might be a little nouveau riche were brushed aside for practical reasons. It takes deep pockets to keep the roof on the old family château.

The expense of delivering bubbles in a bottle that didn't explode came down thanks to improved technology in the cellar just as incomes rose

Above: The rosy-cheeked Madame de Pompadour, Louis XV's mistress, was a tremendous fan of champagne and claimed it was the only wine that left a woman feeling more beautiful.

Opposite (left): From an early affiliation with hot-air balloons, champagne progressed to powered flight. This poster promoted the first true aviation meeting on the plains north of Reims in 1909.

Opposite (right): Pierre Bonnard's famous poster with its frothing tide of fizz appeared all over Paris in the spring of 1891.

among the new middle classes. When the two met in the middle, in the latter half of the nineteenth century, champagne took off. There was no better way to announce you had 'arrived' than that explosive pop of a champagne cork. This was a universal truth from Bristol to Baltimore, but there was something very French about the way the drink was sold. Brands may have been by appointment to royalty and have fancy coats of arms on their labels, but the market was the burgeoning bourgeoisie. French tastes in fashion, above all in food and drink, were what middle-class consumers deferred to all over the world.

While the word *champagne* is masculine in French, it was the country's women who were recruited to advertise the brands, employing all their sex appeal. Today you are not allowed to imply any alcoholic drink might boost your prowess in the bedroom, least of all in France with its draconian *Loi Évin*, but rules were more relaxed in the past. Alongside heroic figures like Jean of Arc and Marianne, the symbol of the French Republic, were an endless cast of *femmes fatales*. They were sophisticated, worldly wise and full of seductive charm. For men, those wicked bubbles might help to loosen a bodice or two, while for women, champagne was the only wine that left you feeling more beautiful, according to Louis XV's mistress, Madame de Pompadour.

Champagne almost became too universal, and it took the combined muscle of the CIVC, and its predecessors, along with the French state, to fully protect its name from all those seeking to use it elsewhere in France and beyond. With total sales now over €6 billion a year, it is the country's top food and drink export, accounting for one-third of all French wine shipments by value. As protected appellations go, its success is on a par with Scotch whisky. Other French wines have struggled due to domestic consumption halving in the space of a generation and the advent of competition from the New World, while champagne resolutely sails on.

Champagne has seeped into every moment of celebration from the most intimate to the most public, from a quiet, family christening to the baptism of a towering new liner. While the location might be some shipyard on the other side of the world, a little piece of France will come swinging through the air to burst against the hull as the ship slips into the water. The idea of launching such a vessel with a bottle of cava or prosecco would be quite unthinkable.

With a good 150 years of practice, the drink has helped the French perfect the art of luxury goods marketing like no one else. And none more so than the mighty LVMH, or Louis Vuitton Moët Hennessy, whose champagne brands include Krug, Dom Pérignon and Veuve Clicquot. As the American wine economist, Mike Veseth, observed: "Champagne is famous, because it isn't really just wine. It is really fame (and luxury) itself."

CHAMPAGNE IN ART AND LITERATURE

An early passage from *The Great Gatsby* finds narrator Nick Carraway drawn to his Long Island neighbour. Later in F. Scott Fitzgerald's great American novel, the fizz still flows, but Carraway detects a sour note has crept in while observing one of Gatsby's parties from the inside.

Carraway first noted: "There was music from my neighbour's house through the summer nights. In his blue gardens men and girls came and went like moths among the whisperings and the champagne and the stars." Later, however:

> *"There were the same people, or at least the same sort of people, the same profusion of champagne, the same many-colored, many-keyed commotion, but I felt an unpleasantness in the air, a pervading harshness that hadn't been there before."*

It was the 1920s, with the Jazz Age in full swing, even if America was theoretically dry due to Prohibition. What else but champagne could reflect the glamour and status of this dazzling socialite who was rumoured to have made his fortune as a bootlegger? The truth is, no other drink packs the same symbolic punch, and for novelists it has always been shorthand for opulence, decadence and excess. When Evelyn Waugh satirised Oxford's Bullingdon club in *Decline and Fall*, he called it "the Bollinger club" and filled it with "the upper classes braying for the sound of broken glasses".

Champagne has allure even for those selling it. In Arthur Miller's *Death of a Salesman*, Willy Loman's son Happy tries to impress a girl in a restaurant by telling her: "I sell champagne, and I'd like you to try my brand." Then, having asked the waiter to bring her a glass, he says she ought to be on the cover of a magazine, before adding: "You know what they say in France, don't you? Champagne is the drink of the complexion ..." As the audience, we know it's all complete fantasy, as Happy's real job is assistant to the assistant buyer at the local store.

Oscar Wilde couldn't resist mentioning his favourite champagne, Perrier-Jouët, in *The Importance of Being Earnest*, and even had a case of it delivered to his cell after his conviction for 'the love that dare not speak its name'. And when ordering one last glass on his deathbed in 1900, he allegedly turned to his doctor, and sighed: "Alas, I am dying beyond my means."

The Russian playwright, Anton Chekhov, followed suit when he died four years later, as his wife recorded in a letter: "... he picked up the glass, turned to me, smiled his wonderful smile and said: 'It's been such a long time since I've had champagne.' He drank it all to the last drop, quietly lay on his left side and was soon silent forever."

Of countless other literary mentions, among the best is this pearl of wisdom from Graham Greene in *Travels with My Aunt*.

> *"Champagne, if you are seeking the truth, is better than a lie detector. It encourages a man to be expansive, even reckless, while lie detectors are only a challenge to tell lies successfully."*

Earlier, Aunt Augusta explains the virtues of flying first class to Paris, because "you can guzzle all the free champagne and make up the difference in cost."

Perhaps there are fewer champagne references in art, but the time and place to look for them is *fin-de-siècle* Paris when Post-Impressionist painters like Pierre Bonnard were in town. It was winning a competition to produce an advertising poster entitled 'France Champagne' in 1889 that encouraged Bonnard to abandon a career in the law and become an artist. The famous lithograph was reproduced all over Paris and inspired many others. All manner of pre-Raphaelite beauties began to appear in prints to promote different brands of champagne.

The English artist Walter Crane painted an allegorical female figure to advertise the long-forgotten Champagne House of Hau & Co. She is entwined with vines in golden, autumnal colours, a jug on her shoulder and holding a champagne *coupe* in an outstretched hand. Meanwhile the Czech painter and decorative artist Alphonse Mucha worked for Hiedsieck and Moët & Chandon at the turn of the century. For the latter he depicted a brunette with a high-necked dress and ornate jewellery to capture the essence of Moët's dry Imperial. For the brand's White Star, Mucha chose a sensual blonde with bare shoulders in a pink dress.

Bonnard's lithograph also inspired his friend Henri de Toulouse-Lautrec to create equally vivid prints, famously in his series for the Moulin Rouge when it flung open its doors at the foot of Montmartre in 1889. While less directly connected with champagne, and with a personal penchant for absinthe in good artistic tradition, Toulouse-Lautrec's art came to symbolise the city at night. As a cabaret venue, the Moulin Rouge was an iconic institution during the period that offered a cocktail of risqué sophistication. Champagne soaked up this imagery of Parisian nightlife and beamed it back around the world. The drink both fuelled the Belle Époque and fed off its image.

The other great Parisian venue was the Folies-Bergère, which opened 20 years earlier, and this was the subject of Édouard Manet's last major work in 1882 and one of his finest. *A Bar at the Folies-Bergère* features a sad-eyed barmaid in front of a giant mirror that plays an optical trick with the viewer. She seems to be staring into space, until we realise from the mirror she is engaged with a shadowy figure in a top hat. In front of her are bottles of champagne on one side and a bowl of oranges on the other. The fruit signifies she is a prostitute.

Opposite: Working in Paris at the turn of the century, Czech artist Alphonse Mucha transformed the art of the poster. These classic lithographs for Moët are a great example.

Below (left): The gleaming gold-topped bottles of champagne in the foreground and the vast chandelier in the mirror suggest opulent glamour in Édouard Manet's *A Bar at the Folies-Bergère*, but the barmaid's eyes say something else.

Below (right, top): Oscar Wilde had a thing about Perrier-Jouët. He even had a case delivered to his cell when he began his prison sentence in 1895.

Bottom (right, bottom): Like Oscar Wilde, only four years later, Anton Chekhov died with the taste of champagne on his lips.

Right: The famous music hall song premiered in the Princess' Concert Hall in Leeds in the summer of 1866.

Opposite: Ariana Grande released 'Pink Champagne' in a YouTube video for her 10 million Twitter fans in 2013.

AG
AG
AG

CELLULOID CHAMPAGNE

The power of champagne to convey glamour, decadence and wealth has long been a gift to filmmakers. The wine's vivacity and sparkle were somehow made for the silver screen, which also benefits from the evocative pop of the cork.

The camera can pull back to take in the champagne-swilling guests at a party, or zoom in to capture the bubbles dancing in a glass. As for sound, audiences had to imagine the pop in Alfred Hitchcock's silent movie *Champagne*, released in 1928 just before the advent of the 'talkies'. It opens and closes with a shot through the bottom of a giant champagne glass that the director had specially made. The film claimed to have "a light, frivolous, frothy character interspersed with touches of tense drama" giving its star, Betty Balfour, the chance to "display her wonderfully vivacious and appealing personality". The critics disagreed, and Hitch later admitted: "The film had no story to tell."

More successful was the 1937 musical *Champagne Waltz*, co-written by Billy Wilder, followed by Greta Garbo's first full-length comedy *Ninotchka* in 1939, where she plays a stern Russian official in Paris who is seduced by a French count with the help of champagne. Having only seen it used to launch Russian battleships, she tells him: "From what I read I thought champagne was a strong drink. It's very delicate," and then, knocking back a glassful, adds: "Do people ever get drunk on this?" Needless to say, she is soon completely legless.

A year later, James Stewart, Cary Grant and Katharine Hepburn teamed up for the beguiling, screwball comedy *The Philadelphia Story*. In one scene, Stewart, playing a prickly journalist, is the most elegant drunk ever to appear on screen. He swerves into Grant's driveway by car one night and emerges clutching a bottle and a paper cup. "Cinderella's slipper," he declares. "It's called champagne. Champagne is a great leveller. It makes you my equal."

And then came *Casablanca*, the ultimate romantic drama in which champagne has a small walk-on part. "Henri wants us to finish this bottle, then three more," says Rick Blaine (Humphrey Bogart) to Ilsa Lund (Ingrid Bergman). "He says he'll water his garden with champagne before he lets the Germans drink any of it." The film came out in 1942, while the Nazis were busy importing as much as possible via their *weinführer* in Reims, Otto Klaebisch.

After the war, the warm embrace between champagne and the movies became more transactional. The studio moguls needed fizz, but they soon sussed the brand-owners would pay for the privilege, such was the glamour of Hollywood and the competition among the Champagne Houses. And on this score, no franchise could match 007. Ian Fleming

Above: "Here's looking at you, kid" – Ingrid Bergman stares deep into Humphrey Bogart's eyes in the 1942 classic *Casablanca*.

Opposite: A multi-tasking James Bond (Sean Connery) beds Jill Masterton (Shirley Eaton) in *Goldfinger*, while checking if the Dom Pérignon is at the right temperature

liked Taittinger, and this was his hero's preferred sparkler in the books. But the brand's film career was cut short in 1963, when a glass was spiked with poison in *From Russia with Love*. Claude Taittinger allegedly refused to have any further involvement with the Broccoli clan. Dom Pérignon stepped in, prompting some of the worst lines in the series. "My dear girl, there are some things that just aren't done, such as drinking Dom Pérignon '53 above the temperature of 38 degrees Fahrenheit," says an insufferably priggish, patronising Bond in *Goldfinger*. "That's just as bad as listening to the Beatles without earmuffs!"

By the time *Live and Let Die* appeared in 1973, Bollinger had oiled its way in and has never looked back. Soon the cheesy double-entendres were coming thick and fast with Roger Moore in the title role. "Bollinger?" he says with a smirk to CIA agent Holly Goodhead in *Moonraker*. "If it's the '69, you were expecting me." This play on vintages became an easy way to separate the goodies from the baddies. In *A View to a Kill*, Bond, takes a sip of champagne and declares it to be Bollinger '75, which impresses detective Achille Aubergine (played by Jean Rougerie) no end. "I see you are a connoisseur." This is all it takes to convince the ridiculous-sounding Frenchman that Bond is who he says he is.

Looking back, it appears the series was rescued just in time before it disappeared into a black hole of self-parody. But such are the costs of production; brands are hired and fired on the set of James Bond. Heineken's 'blink and you'll miss it' appearance in *Skyfall* apparently covered nearly 30% of the film's £98 million production budget. Cynics may wonder if today's scriptwriters simply type in the word 'drink' whenever 007 needs to slake his thirst, and the slot is later auctioned to the highest bidder. If you ever catch Bond bedding down with a bottle of Buckfast you'll know why.

In 1992, the champagne industry must have been delighted by the American comedy *Wayne's World*. "I don't believe I've ever had French champagne before," says Cassandra (Tia Carrere) at one point. "Oh, actually all champagne is French; it's named after the region. Otherwise, it's sparkling white wine," replies Benjamin Oliver (Rob Lowe). The CIVC couldn't have put it better.

Back in the 1920s, novelists like the champagne-loving F. Scott Fitzgerald never mentioned any particular brand in their books. But in Baz Luhrmann's 2013 remake of *The Great Gatsby*, the production designer Catherine Martin decided it had to be Moët & Chandon that flowed through pyramid fountains of glasses and poured from giant-sized bottles. Nothing speaks of wealth and excess quite like a Balthazar or Nebuchadnezzar of champagne. LVMH, the owners of the brand, were naturally delighted, though what the agreement was with Warner Bros. is a closely guarded secret.

More recently, champagne has taken centre stage. In the lavish *Widow Clicquot* from 2024, "Haley Bennett wafts prettily through the film as the young widow of the heir to the Clicquot vineyard," wrote the critic Wendy Ide who dismissed it as "all syrup and no astringency". While in *Sparkling: The Story of Champagne* in 2021, director/narrator Frank Mannion toured the big Houses to record their marketing spiel, until Covid forced him to retreat and cover English fizz instead for the rest of the film. There is a great movie to be made about champagne, but this wasn't it. Then again, perhaps on screen as in life, the drink is best playing a support role with all the effervescent, mood-enhancing charm it can muster.

Left: Hitchcock's 1928 silent film *Champagne* lacked sparkle according to the critics. For the American entertainment magazine *Variety* it was: "an excuse for covering 7,000 feet of harmless celluloid with legs and close-ups."

Above: Unlike F Scott Fitzgerald's book, Baz Luhmann's 2013 film version of *The Great Gatsby* is awash with branded champagne, specifically Moët & Chandon.

Opposite: *Widow Cliquot* (2023) explores the story behind the Veuve Cliquot family.

VISITING CHAMPAGNE

Champagne has always been the most accessible wine region, traipsed over by merchants, pilgrims and foreign aggressors from Attila the Hun to the Nazis. Today's visitors come in peace to soak up the pastoral landscape and above all the wine, in a region that enjoys UNESCO World Heritage status.

Emerging from the mouth of the Channel Tunnel on the French side, it is a comfortable three-hour drive to the heart of Champagne. A train can whisk you from London to Paris or Lille direct to Épernay or Reims in just under four hours on the fastest routes. You can take a fold-up bike on Eurostar, or hire wheels (including e-bikes), when there. Cycling through the vineyards, on minor roads and tracks away from any traffic, has to be one of the best ways to explore the region. For those who prefer to fly, a 30-minute TGV from Paris Charles de Gaulle will take you to Reims (note: it is roughly pronounced 'raance', with a soft 'n', and not 'reems').

Reims is the commercial hub of the region and home to a bevy of Champagne Houses, including Pommery, Ruinart, Krug and Taittinger. There are said to be a billion bottles, give or take, quietly undergoing a secondary fermentation in the maze of subterranean cellars beneath the streets. It makes you wonder – a slight tectonic shift and Reims would collapse through the earth's crust in a crescendo of exploding glass.

The city's Roman entrance to the north – the Porte de Mars – still stands, as does its restored Gothic cathedral of Notre-Dame de Reims and the Jesuit college to the south, but the German artillery flattened almost everything else in between during the First Word War. Rebuilt with art deco flourishes in the 1920s and with a restored cathedral, Reims inevitably lacks the history of other local medieval towns. On the plus side it has some of the best-preserved Gallo-Roman tunnels, especially at Taittinger. Look out for the impressive bas-relief carvings in the cellars of Pommery, whose old family mansion has been transformed into swanky boutique hotel Les Crayères. By night the bars of this university city spark into life, and you can eat well right up to the clutch of Michelin-starred restaurants.

The unofficial 'capital of champagne' is Épernay, half an hour by train south of Reims, almost one-eighth the size and prettier. Here there is no escaping fizz, especially if you strut down the Avenue de Champagne where the HQs of the big Houses vie to outdo each other. The château-style Pol Roger at No. 44 was dubbed "the most drinkable address in Europe" by its greatest fan: Sir Winston Churchill. Jean-Rémy Moët, not content with just one palace, built a replica across the street, known as *La Résidence Trianon*, for Napoleon and his entourage when they headed east. Between Moët & Chandon at No. 20 and Pol Roger lie Mercier and Perrier-Jouët, all of which you can visit for a guided tour of around €30 with a glass of bubbly thrown in.

With some Houses you can just turn up, others you have to book and a few are too grand to open their doors), but you should do one such visit before venturing out into the villages. This is where the real joy of Champagne lies and if you stay in a *gîte* run by a grower-producer – and many do B&B on the side – you will feel much more like a native. In markets like the UK, dominated by perhaps a dozen big brands, the choice of champagne in Champagne is mind-blowing. But help is at hand if you go to: www.vignerons-independent-champagne.com, which narrows the field to 400 or so. Most will happily show you round, give you a little tasting and sell you some fizz, which is just how the Parisians buy their champagne. Their logo – a woodcut of a grower with a barrel on his back – is easy to spot. Springtime can be beautiful as can October-November when the slopes are bathed in reddish gold, but try to avoid late summer when these grower-producers will be too busy with the harvest to welcome visitors.

You can avoid Reims and Épernay altogether and make an appointment at one of the other Grande Marques like Bollinger in Aÿ or Joseph Perrier in Châlons-en-Champagne, as well as local grower-producers. Alternatively, you can head south to arguably the prettiest part of the region and the rolling countryside of the the Côte des Bars, also known as the Aube. The region's capital, with a direct train from Paris, is the half-timbered, almost Bavarian-like town of Troyes. You may not find the glitz and glamour of Épernay's Grands Marques, but possibly something more authentic.

A good starting point is: www.champagne.fr/en/visit-champagne, and for the Aube: www.tourisme-en-champagne.co.uk/cote-des-bar.

WORLD HERITAGE STATUS FOR CHAMPAGNE

In early July 2015, "the vineyards, cellars and champagne houses" were granted World Heritage status by UNESCO, the United Nations' cultural arm. It was one of 11 sites around the world, including the Botanic Gardens of Singapore and Iran's ancient city of Susa. For the Champenois it was a sweet victory and the culmination of a long campaign. UNESCO's rules permit each country to submit only two candidates a year. Champagne had failed to make the grade on its last attempt two years earlier.

Apparently, UNESCO had been particularly impressed by the vineyards of Aÿ and Mareuil-sur-Aÿ and the chalk cellars dug into the St Niçaise hill in Reims during Gallo-Roman times. At the same time parts of Burgundy were also declared a World Heritage site, joining wine regions including Portugal's Douro valley, Tokaj in Hungary and the Mosel valley in Germany.

It was a vindication of how much has changed since the 1980s, when the vineyards were drenched with chemical sprays to kill off bugs and boost yields in a desperate bid to match demand. Since the Millennium a more sustainable approach has been adopted, and the wine's ruling body, the CIVC, has demanded that all vineyards be certified in some way by 2030.

Opposite: Château Les Crayères, Reims.

Below: An arial photograph taken in September 2024 near Pierry and Epernay, eastern France, showing vineyards during the champagne harvest.

Overleaf: There are no shortage of well-signed tourist trails through the region, linking the famous champagne villages.

D 40
ERNAY
Route touristique du
CHAMPAGNE
MANCY

A SPARKLING INVESTMENT

Champagne is for drinking, but some bottles are so rare their owners display them behind glass like precious jewels, or keep them hidden in a bonded warehouse and trade them for profit.

In 2025 you could pop into Aldi and buy a bottle of Veuve Monsigny NV champagne for £14.99 ($19). Produced by Philizot & Fils, it offers a "floral palate, fresh with little development but beautiful balance and restraint", according to the International Wine Challenge, and vies with Moët & Chandon as the country's most popular champagne. Alternatively, you could head for Hedonism Wines in London's Mayfair, where prices reach the dizzy heights of £8,630 ($11,100) for a Methuselah of Dom Perignon Rosé 2003.

This is to illustrate the extremes within the world of champagne. The sparkler from Aldi is very much for drinking, whereas the pink Dom Perignon has other attributes. It is very much at the collectible, investment end of the spectrum, though whether it will increase much further in value is debatable.

If you want to make a killing on champagne, it all depends on when you buy and when you sell, though obviously you first need to pick the right bottles. Those who speculate in fine wine are one leg of a three-legged stool, the others being collectors and well-heeled consumers, though obviously in practice they might be one and the same. If prices rise so high that drinkers and/or collectors are priced out, the stool is liable to collapse. Investors rely on others to diminish the supply by drinking these rarefied bottles and thereby boosting the value of what remains. Luckily for them it seems there are still plenty of extremely rich people out there with an appetite for fizz.

Probably most fancy champagnes sold by merchants like Hedonism will be drunk, perhaps on a Russian yacht. Investors prefer to buy at auction or from fine wine traders and keep their stash in a temperature-controlled bonded warehouse. That way, they are kept safe and sound and free from temptation. Stored under the stairs, it would be all too easy to crack open the bottles in a moment of reckless abandon among friends, though arguably that is precisely what champagne was invented for.

The names to look out for when it comes to 'investment-grade' champagne include Dom Pérignon, Krug, Louis Roederer Cristal, Taittinger Comtes de Champagne, Salon Cuvée 'S' Le Mesnil, Philipponnat Clos des Goisses, plus the top wines of Ruinart, Bollinger and Pol Roger. Pricing relates to the prestige of the House and the scores of the leading critics for the particular release and the vintage. But as in Bordeaux, producers will be furtively looking over their shoulders to see what their rivals are charging. The release prices represent a form of ranking for the top Houses, and a reaffirmation of their status.

Production of these prestige cuvées tends to be very small. For example, Salon Mesnil releases fewer than 3,000 cases a year, while for Cristal it is fewer than 25,000 cases. The sales are tracked on a weekly basis by Liv-ex, which operates like a mini stock exchange for such wines, which are traded in the secondary market, often via online auctions.

According to a recent report by Liv-ex, champagne accounted for only 2% of the total secondary market for wine in 2012. Within a decade that figure had risen to 12.4%, making it the third most-traded fine wine region after Bordeaux and Burgundy. The report went on to explain that, "speculators rarely drink their stock, meaning that the volumes released with each new vintage no longer diminish at their usual rate."

For would-be investors, Grande Marque champagnes used to offer the same sort of pedigree as a First Growth from Bordeaux for a lot less money, but prices have been catching up fast, reflecting not just increased demand, but the ambition, or possibly greed, of the producers. No bull market lasts forever. The sums paid for the top wines of Bordeaux soared to a peak in 2011, only to crash by a third shortly afterwards.

"Of course, the great advantage of wine is that even if it is not worth as much as it was the year before, it will probably taste better. So, at least you get to drink your investment even if you can't cash it in," claimed Simon Berry, when he was chairman of the blue-chip London wine merchant Berry Bros.

Consumption is clearly not an option for other alternative investments like gold, oil or carbon credits, but knowing that a particular champagne has slumped in value might affect one's appreciation of it. What's that distinctive aroma lurking behind those notes of brioche and toasted almonds, if not the scent of sour grapes?

Opposite (above): Champagne bottles in storage in Marne, France.

Opposite (below): Amber nectar poured from a 200-year-old bottle of champagne in 2010, having been rescued by divers from a shipwreck in the Baltic Sea near the Finnish Åland islands.

AUCTIONS

Along with releases like the Krug Collection, dribbled out on to the secondary market, are really old, rare bottles that crop up at auction. Their value will be affected by the reliability of their provenance, and the condition they are in, although exceptions are made. In 2010, divers exploring a shipwreck off the Åland Islands, in the Baltic Sea, discovered a stash of champagne bottles dating from the 1820s. The labels had long disintegrated, but from the corks three were identified with "absolute certainty" as Veuve Clicquot, whose then winemaker Francis Hautekeur was lucky enough to try some. He claimed it had "a toasty, zesty nose with hints of coffee and a very agreeable taste, with accents of flowers and lime". A bottle of this ancient Veuve Clicquot sold at auction in New York in 2011 for US$43,630 (£26,675/€30,400) – a world-record price for champagne until eclipsed by a bottle of 1874 Perrier Jouët, that went for £42,875 at Christies in London a decade later.

INDEX

D

E

F

G

H

I

J

CREDITS

The publishers would like to thank the following sources for their kind permission to reproduce the pictures in this book.

The Advertising Archives: 103TR, 105T

akg-images: 42; Les Arts Décoratifs, Paris / Jean Tholance 80T, 80B

Alamy Stock Photo: allOver images 60-61; Archivart 140L, 140R; Greg Balfour Evans 15T; BFA 147; Bon Appetit 116R; Michael Busselle/Robert Harding 110R; Capi-Chef 34; Paul Collis 75L; Iaroslav Danylchenko 8-9; Jean-Pierre Degas/Hemis 52; DGDImages 132T; Julian Eales 111R; Claire Evans 23B; Per Karlsson/BKWine.com 99T; Christophe Lepetit/Only France 98; Lordprice Collection 22, 75R, 89T, 115R; Andrew Matthews/ PA Images 130; David Noble/nobleIMAGES 58B; North Wind Picture Archives 35; Pictorial Press Ltd 146R; Jorn Pilon 77T; Gillian Pullinger 131L; Teofil Rewers 131R; Bertrand Rieger/Hemis 26; Robert Harding 48B; Olivier Roux/Sagaphoto 68, 76; Daniele Schneider/Photononstop 16; Smith Archive 90; Richard Soberka/Hemis 106, 116L; SS Studios 23T

Champagne Billecart-Salmon: 54, 55TL, 55TR, 55BL, 55BR

Bridgeman Images: Estate of Gerald Bloncourt 48T; Look and Learn 79B; Look and Learn/Barbara Loe Collection 71TR; The Stapleton Collection 13T, 13B, 14, 81T

Champagnes & Châteaux Canard Duchêne: 109L

Cephas Picture Library: Mick Rock 17R, 18, 25, 71TL, 117R

G.H. Mumm: 21, 82L, 82C, 82R, 83BL, 83BR

Getty Images: AFP 88B; Sergi Alexander 107; Apic 43; Pierre Beauvillain/ AFP 149; Bettmann 46; Clive Brunskill 51; Carl Court 133; DEA/G. Dagli Orti/De Agostini 31; Mark Downey Lucid Images/Corbis 143; Bruno Ehrs 104L; Pepe Franco/Cover 125T; Owen Franken 117L; David Goddard 132B; Tim Graham 94R, 111L; Karl Hendon 112-113; Hulton Archive 30R; Alain Julien/AFP 6; LMPC 146L; Alastair Miller/Bloomberg 20T; Thierry Monasse 153T; Jonathan Nackstrand/AFP 153B; Francois Nascimbeni/ AFP 28, 104R, 109R; Philippe Petit/Paris Match 23T; PHAS/Universal Images Group 29R; Paul Popper/Popperfoto 74; Popperfoto 145; The Print Collector 32, 36, 37T; Chris Ratcliffe/Bloomberg 134-135; Ilya S. Savenok 123R; Lucas Schifres/Bloomberg 49; Science & Society Picture Library 139L; Sepia Times/Universal Images Group 40; Marco Serena/NurPhoto 118; Paul Slade/Paris Match 88C; Pakin Songmor 12; Sylvain Sonnet 47; Ben Stansall/AFP 126L; Oliver Strewe 148; Universal History Archive/ Universal Images Group 44L; Wilatlak Villette 11; Warner Brothers 144

Champagne Gosset: 62L, 62R, 63T, 63BL, 63BR

Jacquart & Associés Distribution: 115L

Champagne Jacquesson: 66L, 66R, 67T, 67BL, 67BR

Champagne Joseph Perrier: 69T, 69BL, 69BR

Champagne Lanson: 72, 73TL, 73TR, 73BL, 73BR

Laurent-Perrier: 77BL, 77BR

Limm Communications Ltd.: 64T, 64B, 65T, 65BL, 65BR

Champagne Mailly Grand Cru: 114

Maisons Marques et Domaines: 19T, 19B, 24, 94L, 95BL, 95BR, 96-97

Mary Evans Picture Library: 56R, 83T; Grenville Collins Postcard Collection 45; The Roseries Collection 29L

Mentzendorff & Co.: 56L, 57T, 57BL, 57BR, 110L

Moët Hennessy: 33L, 33R, 37B, 58T, 59T, 59BL, 59BR, 70L, 70R, 71BL, 71BR, 78, 79T, 81BL, 81BR, 99C, 99BL, 99BR, 101, 105BL, 105BR, 108L, 108R, 136

Perrier-Jouët: 84TL, 84TR, 84B, 85T, 85BL, 85BR

Champagne Philipponnat: 50, 86L, 86R, 87T, 87BL, 87BR

Piper-Heidsieck: 89BL, 89BR

Pol Roger: 20B, 91TL, 91TR, 91BL, 91BR

Private Collection: 41

Réunion des Musées Nationaux: 38, 39

Shutterstock: Joan Bautista 124; Claudio Giovanni Colombo 15B; Everett Collection 141TR, 141BR; FiledIMAGE 127; gg-foto 128-129; Alessandro Guerriero 121; Jag_cz 154-155; Daan Kloeg 150-151; Lusia83 122; Rosangela Perry 126R; Alessia Pierdomenico 123L; Joe Schildhorn/BFA 95T; Zryzner 125B

Champagne Tattinger: 17L, 102T, 102B, 103TL, 103BL, 103BR

Vranken-Pommery Monopole: 92L, 92R, 93T, 93BL, 93BR

Wikimedia Commons: 30L, 30C, 44R, 88T, 100, 120, 138, 139R, 141L, 142